MEDIEVAL
MERCENARY

Sir John Hawkwood of Essex

MEDIEVAL
MERCENARY

Sir John Hawkwood of Essex

Christopher Starr

ESSEX RECORD OFFICE

Essex Record Office
Chelmsford
2007

Published by the Essex Record Office,
Wharf Road, Chelmsford, Essex CM2 6YT, United Kingdom
© Essex County Council 2007

A catalogue reference for this book is available from the British Library.

ISBN: 978-1-898529-27-9

Essex Record Office Publication Number: 153

Cover illustration *Detail of monumental brass commemorating Sir Robert Swinborne (d.1391), Little Horkesley, Essex.*
Photograph Christopher Starr

The certainty of death is attended with uncertainties, in time, manner, places. The variety of Monuments hath often obscured true graves: and *Centotaphs* confounded Sepulchres. For beside their reall Tombs, many have founded honorary and empty Sepulchres.

Sir Thomas Browne
Hydriotaphia. Urne-Buriall (1658)

This book is dedicated to all the soldiers
with whom I have served.

CONTENTS

FOREWORD

by General Sir Roger Wheeler GCB CBE
Constable of the Tower of London
Former Chief of the General Staff

I am pleased to have been invited to write a foreword to this book about an English soldier and man of Essex.

By any standards, Sir John Hawkwood was an extraordinary soldier. During a military career spanning some fifty-five years he showed himself to be an outstanding leader. In his last battle, at the age of seventy-two, in which he apparently fought in hand-to-hand combat, he secured for his adopted city Florence a great victory against overwhelming odds.

Hawkwood evidently had many unusual and outstanding qualities, both as a soldier and as a commander. He was also, despite his long absence from England, a patriot who earned the admiration of his king and the nobility for his military prowess and his diplomatic skills. Interestingly he was an able exponent of military intelligence, using 'spies' to collect information about terrain, enemy formations and morale. He also employed what would now be termed psychological operations, to confuse or perhaps confound his opponents. His use of astrologers in this context is rather more suspect.

Clearly, Hawkwood was the master of the battlefield. He employed combined arms – cavalry, infantry and archers – to achieve victory, and he was prepared to try out unusual tactics and weapons in the course of his campaigns. Of particular importance is his success in commanding a multi-national army comprising soldiers from many parts of Europe. He was renowned for his loyalty, not only to his employers but also to the soldiers who served with him. They, in return, responded with unusual fidelity and it seems that his personal bodyguard of archers served him throughout his career in Italy.

Hawkwood was undoubtedly a charismatic man whose leadership inspired his men to acts of great courage and endurance. He was, ultimately, perhaps the most skilful and successful *condottiere* of his time. His great military virtues should not, however, blind us to his vices. Who could not but condemn his involvement in the massacres at Cesena and Faenza?

I believe that the author has written an evenly balanced view of Hawkwood the soldier and in addition has shown us the man in his Essex context. At the end of his life, Sir John Hawkwood made careful plans to return to his native county and, I think, we can assume that is where his heart really lay.

Roger Wheeler

ACKNOWLEDGEMENTS

The genesis of this book lies in a cycle ride I made in July 1962 to Sible Hedingham church to see the monument described in my well-used copy of Pevsner's *Essex* as "considered to be the cenotaph for Sir John Hawkwood". It also follows many visits to the Essex Record Office where, from the age of fourteen, I have been patiently guided through its manuscripts sources by its incomparable staff.

I take great pleasure in acknowledging the extraordinary help I have received from many *well-wishers* who include my family, friends, scholars, archivists and custodians of churches and houses, in this country and in Italy: Dr David Andrews, Mr Michael Beale, Mr Geoffrey Beastall, Dr Eve Borsook, Ms Ann Bowen, Mr and Mrs Ian Carruthers, Mr James Christie, Dr Linda Clark, Miss Susan Clark, Dr Janet Cooper, Mrs Nancy Edwards, Contessa Orietta Floridi, Professor Kenneth Fowler, Professor Harold Fox, (the late) Mr John and Mrs Hill, Mr Terry Jones, Mr William Liddell, Dr Philip Morgan, Professor Gigliola Pagano de Divitiis, Dr David Postles, Mr W. Raymond Powell, Professor Nigel Saul, Miss Janet Smith, Mrs Jutta Starr, Mr Martin Stutchfield, Dr Christopher Thornton, Signore Luigi Troiano, Dr Jennifer Ward, General Sir Roger Wheeler, Mr Roderick Wright and Mr Robert Yorke.

I would also like to place on record my thanks to the Friends of Historic Essex for their generous financial contribution to the printing costs of this book. I am most grateful to Ms Deborah Peers for seeing *Medieval Mercenary* through each stage of its production from manuscript to printed book, to Clare Banks (Reeve Banks Photography) for her photographs of Hawkwood's Essex and Buffey & Buffey for designing the book.

Finally I would like to thank 22 Company for reasons they will understand but only they need to know.

Christopher Starr
2007

Sir John Hawkwood's tomb, St Peter's Church, Sible Hedingham. Photograph Clare Banks

INTRODUCTION

The exploits of Sir John Hawkwood, otherwise known as Giovanni Acuto, the fourteenth-century mercenary from Sible Hedingham in Essex, are generally well known. However, the historical facts of his life are not always easily distinguished from the myths and legends that have grown up about him and his White Company of soldiers.

Typically, Hawkwood is described as the son of an Essex tanner who, having been apprenticed to a London tailor, enlisted in the English army to fight the French at the beginning of the Hundred Years War.[1] The story goes on to suggest that, after distinguishing himself at the Battles of Crécy and Poitiers, he was knighted by Edward III and subsequently made his way to Italy where he carved out a successful career as a *condottiere* or mercenary captain. He later acquired the soubriquet *diavolo incarnato*, 'the devil incarnate', and was also condemned for his merciless atrocities by the Dominican (later Saint) Catherine of Siena.[2]

There is even a fanciful account of his birth which purports to explain the origin of his surname – he is said to have been born prematurely

The Battle of Crécy, 1346, at which John Hawkwood the younger, later Sir John Hawkwood, is said to have been present.

in a wood after his mother was frightened by a hawk. There are also many tales of his cruelty and ruthlessness as a mercenary; the most extreme of which, after the sack of the town of Cesena, has him cut a captive nun in half so as to prevent two of his soldiers arguing as to who should take possession of her. Another tradition is that some monks gave Hawkwood (whose brother was a poor priest) the greeting 'Peace' to which he replied, 'May the Lord take away your alms'. Hawkwood's reply took them by surprise and they explained that they had only meant well. The warrior's icy response was, 'Don't you realise that I make my living by war, and that peace would ruin me?'[3]

Attempts to locate Hawkwood's final resting-place have spawned a great deal of misinformation and speculation. After his death, and burial in the Duomo in Florence, Hawkwood's body is said to have been returned to England at the request of Richard II, and thereafter to have been reinterred in Sible Hedingham church in a tomb paid for by his trustees. A number of writers assert that this tomb was subsequently destroyed and that, in any case, it was never more than a cenotaph.[4] As to his posterity – Hawkwood's youngest son is supposed to have been knighted and ended his days at Sible Hedingham, whilst one of his daughters is the reputed ancestor of the poet Shelley.

There is undoubtedly an element of truth in some of these stories and, in order to reveal the facts about Hawkwood, this book examines surviving records concerning his ancestry, his close family, his kin, friends and associates. Although a brief outline of his military career is also described in Chapter 1, those wishing to follow this aspect of

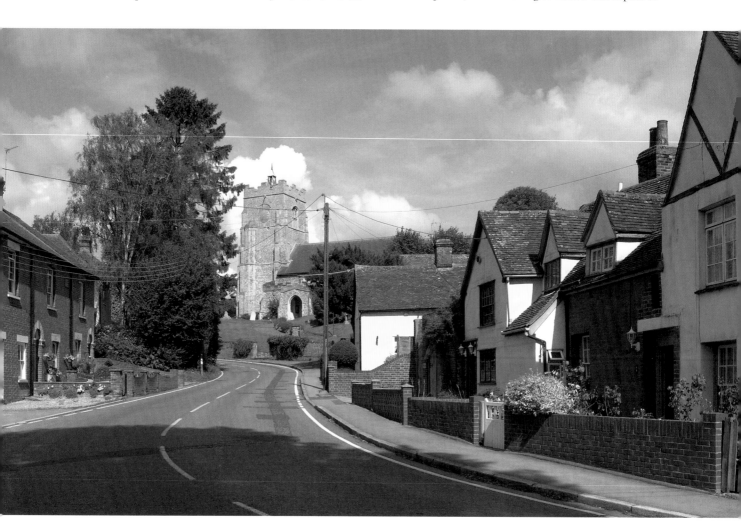

Sible Hedingham, St Peter's Parish Church in the background. Photograph Clare Banks

Hawkwood's life in greater depth are directed to the bibliography. The present work describes Sir John Hawkwood, a national and international figure, in his local context, and is essentially a work of English local history. It employs most of the known sources of material contained in British archives. There are, however, many hundreds of Hawkwood's letters and other documents in the archives of Florence, Lucca, Pisa and other Italian cities, and his definitive biography has yet to be written.[5]

In British records Sir John Hawkwood can occasionally be difficult to distinguish from certain other members of his family, as his older brother, nephew and two of his sons were also named John Hawkwood. In Italy things were simpler – he was generally known by the nickname *Acuto*, 'the sharp one'. When Italians did attempt to spell his surname in contemporary sources it emerged variously as 'Haukutd', 'Haucbbod', 'Hauckwood', 'Haucud', 'Hauchud' and so on – but there is little doubt to whom they referred.

THE HAWKWOODS OF SIBLE HEDINGHAM & GOSFIELD

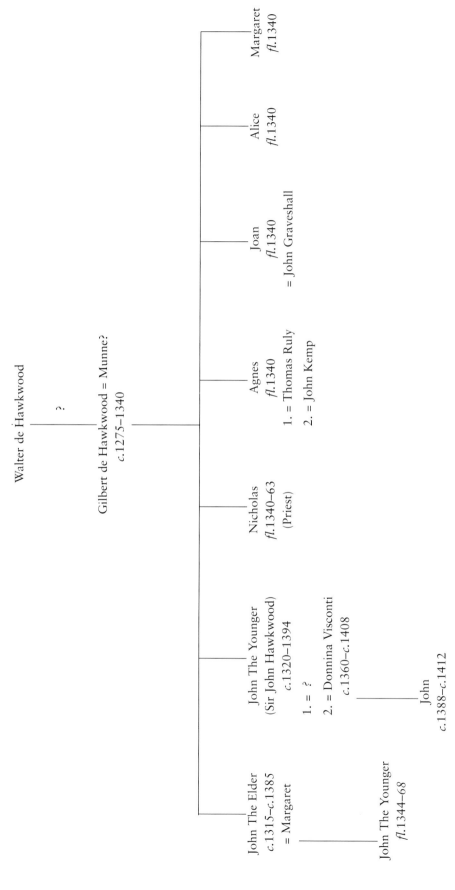

Walter de Hawkwood

?

Gilbert de Hawkwood = Munne?
c.1275–1340

John The Elder
c.1315–c.1385
= Margaret

John The Younger
(Sir John Hawkwood)
c.1320–1394

1. = ?

2. = Donnina Visconti
c.1360–c.1408

Nicholas
fl.1340–63
(Priest)

Agnes
fl.1340
1. = Thomas Ruly
2. = John Kemp

Joan
fl.1340
= John Graveshall

Alice
fl.1340

Margaret
fl.1340

John The Younger
fl.1344–68

John
c.1388–c.1412

Family tree of the Hawkwoods.

CHAPTER ONE

Hawkwood's CAREER

Sir John Hawkwood was the son of Gilbert de Hawkwood of Sible Hedingham, and was born there *c.*1320, or perhaps at Gosfield where his father also had property. Nothing is known about his mother or his earliest years, but according to his father's will dated 18 July 1340, he was to be given his keep for a year by his brother John Hawkwood the elder, together with a quantity of grain, a bed and the substantial sum of twenty pounds.[6] Why the infant John's parents had him christened with the same name as his older brother we do not know, but this confusing practice was not uncommon at the time; each child probably took his name from one of his godfathers.

Sible Hedingham is a large parish of some 5365 acres; probably much the same size as it was in the early fourteenth century, and is situated in the Hinckford hundred of north-west Essex. The parish is contiguous with Great Yeldham, Castle Hedingham, Great Maplestead,

Halstead, Gosfield, Wethersfield and Toppesfield – and only a thin strip of land separates it from nearby Finchingfield. In Gilbert de Hawkwood's time there were five manors in the parish: Prayors (otherwise Bower Hall), Grave's Hall, Grey's Hall, Bloy's Hall, and Glasscocks – to give them their modern spelling.[7] The village lay adjacent to the great *caput* of the de Vere family, earls of Oxford, at Castle Hedingham – the castle being clearly visible from the Hawkwoods' substantial house in Potter Street.[8] The de Veres exercised considerable influence throughout the county, not least in the villages closest to their castle. So too did the Bourchier family seated at their more modest estate in Halstead. The de Veres and Bourchiers alternated as patrons of the benefice of Sible Hedingham church and it was a member of the latter family, John de Bousser, rector until *c.*1336, who may have baptised John Hawkwood and his siblings in St Peter's Church.[9] The Bourchiers held the manor of Prayors in Sible Hedingham but they were not permanently

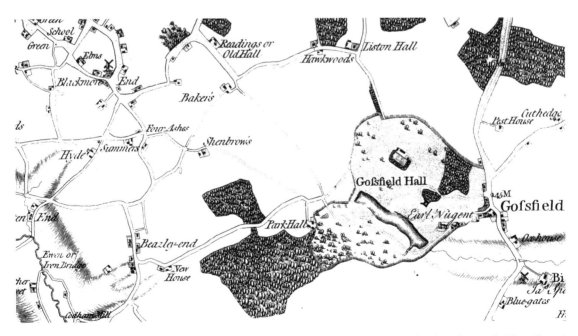

Gosfield. Chapman and André's map of 1777 showing St Katherine's Parish Church, Gosfield Hall and Hawwwood's Farm (from a copy in the Essex Record Office).

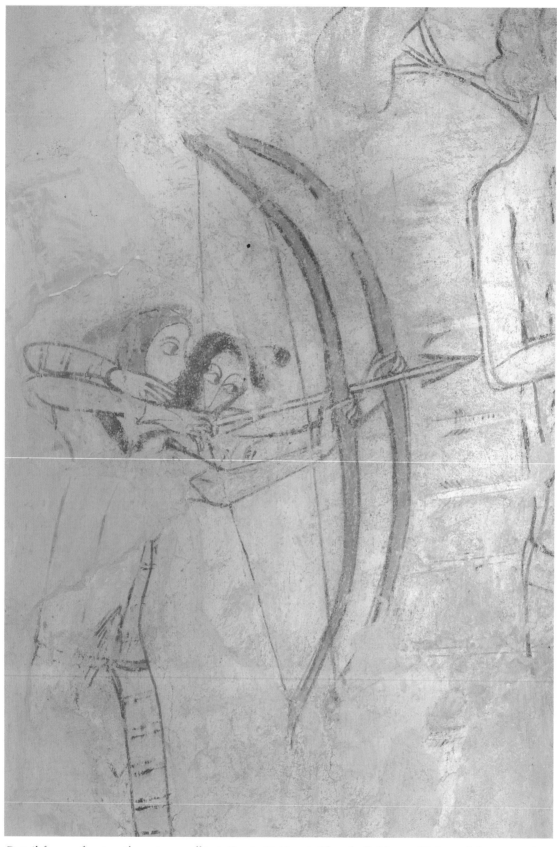

Detail from a fourteenth-century wall painting in St Mary's Church, Belchamp Walter, of the martyrdom of St Edmund. In Hawkwood's time the longbow was a battle-winning weapon for the English army.

Photograph Clare Banks

Hedingham Castle, home of the de Vere earls of Oxford. It may have been here that John Hawkwood enlisted as a soldier at the beginning of the Hundred Years War. ERO: I/Mp 90/3/1/29

resident in the village, the keeping of the manor being in the hands of their steward, who may have occupied the manor house.[10]

According to legend (partly fabricated by his earliest Italian biographer) Hawkwood was apprenticed to a tailor; whilst this is possible, it is unlikely in the light of subsequent events.[11] It seems quite probable, however, that c.1340 the young John Hawkwood joined the English army which was then campaigning in France. He may have enlisted at Hedingham Castle in the retinue of John, Earl of Oxford (d.1361), his father's feudal lord, but he could alternatively have joined the retinue of Robert, Lord Bourchier of Halstead (d.1349) or that of John, Lord Fitzwalter of Henham and Woodham Walter (d.1361). These three local members of the higher nobility were all notable soldiers in the army of Edward III.

There has been much speculation about Hawkwood's supposed presence at the Battles of Crécy (1346) and Poitiers (1356), but there is no

evidence that he was there or that he was subsequently knighted by Edward III. Hawkwood was, however, referred to by Jean Froissart in his chronicle of the first phase of the Hundred Years War as a 'poor knight', so it is possible that he was knighted by the King or one of his nobles.[12] It has been further suggested that Hawkwood began his military career as an archer, but this too is merely speculation. He was fortunate to survive not only the war, but also the Black Death that devastated France and later England during 1348 and 1349. His immediate family (quite possibly he had married by this time) might not have been so lucky. In 1360 when the Treaty of Brétigny brought a truce and temporary peace between England and France, Hawkwood was aged about thirty-eight, and may by then have already had some twenty years' experience of combat. With even civilian life expectancy at about forty years, Hawkwood may indeed have considered himself lucky to be alive. Despite this, he was in fact only halfway through his life, and

his greatest achievements were still in the distant future.[13]

Hawkwood was perhaps a disappointed man when fighting ceased in May 1360 - soldiering in the English army was probably his only means of earning a living. As a knight who was the younger son of a very minor member of the gentry, he had apparently risen, through his own efforts, to the present-day equivalent of company or battalion commander. When released from military service in France after the Treaty of Brétigny, he travelled south, along with thousands of other redundant fighting men from England, Wales, France and elsewhere. Following another serious outbreak of plague in France (and England), the Rhône valley appears to have functioned as a base from which this unemployed rabble of individuals and groups of soldiers were channelled towards potentially

Mercenary soldiers in combat, a detail from a fresco commemorating the victory of Sienese forces over English mercenaries in 1363.

Vanni, Lippo (1344-1375): Victory of the Sienese at Sinalunga. Siena, Palazzo Pubblico.
© 1990. Photo Scala, Florence

rich pickings at Avignon, which was at that time the principal residence of the Pope. This hoard of marauders captured nearby Pont-Saint-Esprit, but was somehow bought off at the gates of Avignon by the Pope himself. Thereafter many of them scattered across France and Italy to seek other opportunities for plunder or paid employment; John Hawkwood was a leading figure in the attack on Pont-Saint-Esprit.

During the autumn of 1360 groups and individual soldiers gradually drew together into military formations known as free or great

companies. These companies were led by captains who were either self-appointed or elected by their soldiers. There was no formal structure to the great companies, but they usually comprised a number of subunits called *routes*, or lesser companies, that were commanded by subordinate captains. Below them were marshals and constables. The concept of great companies was not new as they had been operating as mercenaries in Italy for a century or more. Hawkwood reappears in the records in February 1361 as the marshal of such a great company where his experience of command in France had no doubt given him an advantage over most of his fellows.

Later in the same year Hawkwood served under Albert (or Albrecht) Sterz who commanded an Anglo-German company (which was the antecedent of the White Company) that sold its services to the Marquis of Montferrat who was then at war with Milan. Under Sterz, Hawkwood campaigned in Italy against the Count of Savoy, but may have then returned to France in 1362 to take part in the Battle of Brignais on 6 April. This is the last time Hawkwood is known to have travelled outside Italy for, despite his previous long service in the English army, he chose to remain in Italy when war broke out once again between England and France, presumably because he found

Soldiers looting a house. English mercenaries were notoriously difficult to control when fighting was over. Detail from a late fourteenth-century manuscript. Chroniques de France ou de Saint Denis. Roy MS. 20. CV11, fo. 4lv.

it more lucrative to do so and he had no contractual obligation to serve in his country's army again. This decision did not detract from the esteem in which he was to be held later in England, as is evidenced by parliamentary records and a number of contemporary chronicles.[14]

It was after Brignais that Hawkwood's career as an independent mercenary can be said to have really begun. No doubt when he saw how vast sums of money could be obtained by the use of military force, he began to focus his ambitions in that direction. Upon his return from France Hawkwood resumed his service with Sterz, who in April 1363 defeated Milan's fearsome Hungarian troops at Canturino. In the following July Sterz was appointed captain-general of the Pisan army with Hawkwood as one of his subordinate commanders. Having fought for Montferrat against Milan, Hawkwood now found himself fighting on behalf of Pisa, an ally of Milan, against Florence. Such reversals were to be common throughout his career. One mid nineteenth-century

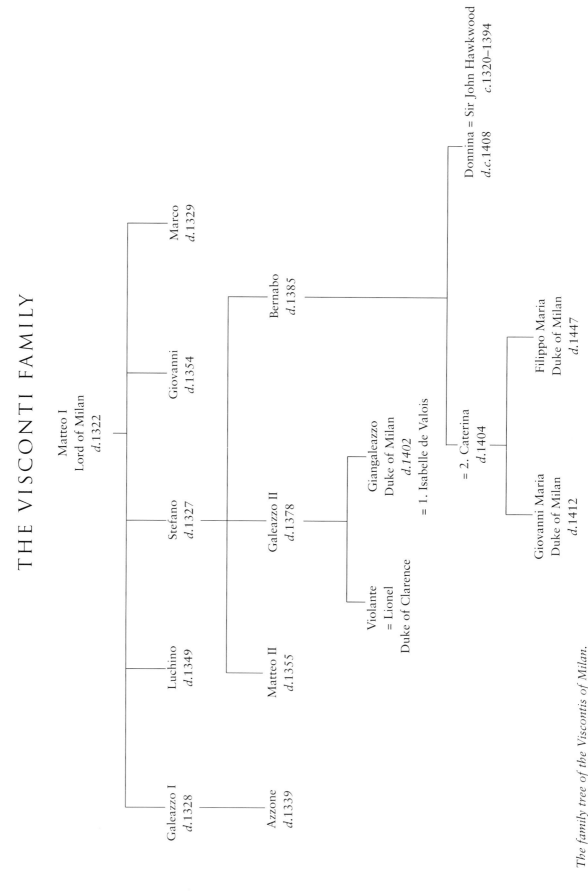

THE VISCONTI FAMILY

Matteo I
Lord of Milan
d.1322

Galeazzo I
d.1328

Luchino
d.1349

Stefano
d.1327

Giovanni
d.1354

Marco
d.1329

Azzone
d.1339

Matteo II
d.1355

Galeazzo II
d.1378

Bernabo
d.1385

Violante
= Lionel
Duke of Clarence

Giangaleazzo
Duke of Milan
d.1402
= 1. Isabelle de Valois

= 2. Caterina
d.1404

Donnina = Sir John Hawkwood
d.c.1408   *c.1320–1394*

Giovanni Maria
Duke of Milan
d.1412

Filippo Maria
Duke of Milan
d.1447

The family tree of the Viscontis of Milan.

author described the phenomenon: 'Nothing could exceed the reckless indifference with which these mercenaries of every nation changed their masters. Not only did the generals pass over from one service to another, but the captains with their troops abandoned the general, and the privates deserted their captains with no more consciousness of treachery than a modern footman feels on leaving his place for better wages'.[15]

By the end of 1363, Hawkwood had taken the place of Sterz as captain-general and Pisa hired still more troops to be placed under Hawkwood's command. The Pisan army invaded Florentine territory and, en route for Florence, suffered several defeats; Hawkwood then retreated to Incisa where he turned the tables and defeated the Florentine army. At this point, most of his men, including the demoted Sterz, deserted, having been bribed to do so by Florence.

Early in 1364, Hawkwood's company (now the White Company) reformed, gained a new contract from Pisa and was rejoined by Sterz. Amongst the White Company's English officers were William Gold and John Thornbury. When pursued and attacked by a reinforced Florentine army, led by the German mercenary Hans von Bongard, Hawkwood retreated to Pisa; he counter-attacked but his troops were defeated with heavy losses. The Florentine army under its captain-general Galeotto Malatesta then took advantage of Pisa's weakness and invaded Pisan territory, eventually sacking the rich port of Livorno. This disastrous defeat led to a revolution in Pisa that brought about the proclamation of the merchant Giovanni dell'Agnello as doge; he soon made peace with Florence and strengthened Pisa's alliance with Milan.

Hawkwood stayed loyal to Pisa throughout these changes of fortune, and loyalty was one of his defining characteristics. Doubtless he learned many lessons in this campaign, having for the first time been exposed to the serial treachery of his fellow mercenaries. At the end of the year, Hawkwood took his soldiers to pillage the Perugino; pillage was to become a habitual indulgence whenever he found himself temporarily without paid employment. To combat the threat from Hawkwood, Perugia

(claimed by the Pope as part of the papal states) hired a company of Germans under Hans von Bongard and when he realised that von Bongard's soldiers were a match for his own, Hawkwood withdrew to Lombardy.

Hawkwood unwisely returned to the Perugino in 1365 and was eventually brought to battle and defeated by von Bongard on 25 July. His adversary pursued him first to Siena, then to Genoa, where Hawkwood and his remaining men joined forces with Ambrogio Visconti (his friend and future brother-in-law) in the Italian Company of St George, together with Count John of Hapsburg and his company of Germans. This partnership continued (with Visconti in command) until the spring of 1366 when Hawkwood and his men returned to the Perugino to ravage the countryside without interference from von Bongard, defeating a Perugian army at Brufa. In 1368, presumably at the invitation of Bernabo Visconti, Hawkwood attended the wedding of Lionel, Duke of Clarence, second son of Edward III, who married Violante, daughter of Galeazzo Visconti, Bernabo's brother. Hawkwood already had links with the Visconti rulers of Milan (power being shared by the brothers Bernabo (d.1385) and Galeazzo (d.1378)) and entered Bernabo's service soon after the wedding. Almost his first task in Visconti's pay was to defend successfully the Milanese fortress of Borgoforte against the forces of Emperor Charles IV.

In 1369, Hawkwood fought on behalf of his recent adversary – Perugia. The city was at war with the Pope but allied with Milan, which sent Hawkwood to lead its forces. On this occasion Hawkwood seriously misjudged the military situation and, in June 1369, was ambushed and captured by the Pope's German mercenaries at Arezzo. He was held prisoner by them until money was raised for his ransom. Once free, Hawkwood repeatedly pillaged the Pope's territories before returning home. In December 1369, Bernarbo Visconti ordered Hawkwood and his forces to attack a Florentine army under the leadership of Giovanni Malatacca. They defeated the Florentines at San Miniato. Visconti then decided to restore the deposed doge, dell'Agnello, to Pisa and sent Hawkwood to attack the city. This attack failed, so Hawkwood took his soldiers on

an opportunist raid and again sacked Livorno. The Florentines soon retaliated and their army attacked and defeated Hawkwood's forces. The result of this bitter struggle between the cities of Florence and Milan was a treaty concluded in November 1370.

It is difficult to see how Hawkwood gave his employers value for money at this stage of his career; his victories were hardly balanced by his defeats. In this situation and at the age of fifty, Hawkwood might reasonably have decided to cut his losses, but perhaps he sensed that his fortunes were about to change. It is worth remembering that at fifty he would have been considered an elderly man, yet he still had some years to go before he reached the high point of his career.

In the summer of 1372, Hawkwood attacked the forces of Lutz von Landau, an ally of the Marquis of Montferrat, and captured him. After this victory Hawkwood at once invaded Montferrat's territory, but the campaign came to nothing. Later that year, probably because his salary was in arrears (as so often happened to the *condottieri*), Hawkwood abandoned the Visconti family and transferred his allegiance to the new Pope. Gregory XI planned to move the papacy from Avignon back to Rome and had declared war on both Milan and Florence (the Anti-Papal League) in what was to become known

Hawkwood's Castello di Montecchio Vesponi which dominates the countryside near Cortona, Tuscany. In private ownership, it is occasionally open to the public. Photographs Christopher Starr

as the War of the Eight Saints. In January 1373 Hawkwood achieved a victory for his new employer, defeating the Milanese on the river Panaro, only to be defeated on 8 May 1373 at Montechiaro by Giangaleazzo Visconti, the Count of Virtue (Bernabo's nephew and eventual successor). Characteristically, Hawkwood soon regrouped his forces and destroyed the Milanese army at Gavardo. A year-long truce began in June 1374, time which Hawkwood seems to have spent in Bologna. Although the Pope was no better in paying his debts than Visconti had been, Hawkwood remained loyal to him.

Despite payment from the Pope being in arrears, it is probable that Hawkwood paid his soldiers from his own resources, and this partially accounts for their loyalty to their commander. Still nominally in the Pope's pay, Hawkwood drifted back to his freelance activities and, in an effort to recoup his losses, ravaged a succession of Tuscan cities. Somehow persuaded to return to the Pope's service in July 1375 as Captain of the Holy Company, he was ordered to march against Tuscany. His new marshals included Sir John Thornbury and William Gold. Thornbury was to become one of Hawkwood's most bitter rivals and eventually his enemy. Stalemate followed in Tuscany because Hawkwood, still unpaid, was disinclined to fight on the Pope's behalf. Disinclined but not disloyal, Hawkwood refused generous offers from Milan, Florence and Venice to desert his employer. Such feelings of loyalty did not weigh heavily with all his troops however, for in August 1375, after fierce disagreements with Hawkwood, Sir John Thornbury defected to Milan. Hawkwood meanwhile took the opportunity to sign a non-aggression agreement with Florence and was granted an annual pension for life. He had probably come to recognise that the financial power wielded by the citizens of Florence was the equal of any other city in Italy, and that his future prosperity lay in being its employee, not its enemy.

The city of Perugia seized this moment to revolt and joined Florence in its conflict with the Pope. Hawkwood made little effort to crush it, instead he took possession of several castles in the Romagna in lieu of his unpaid salary, so becoming one of the first foreign *condottiere* to own land in Italy. Bologna joined in the revolt against the Pope and in

The poet Geoffrey Chaucer whose Knight in the Canterbury Tales is said to be an ironic portrait of his acquaintance Sir John Hawkwood.

the process took Hawkwood's two sons (apparently by his first marriage) as hostages. Eventually, in return for a truce, the city released the young men when their father threatened retribution. Hawkwood vented his anger on Faenza, sacked it, then spent the rest of that year at Cortignola enlarging and strengthening the fortifications of the town and his own castle. At this low point in his career as a mercenary he was perhaps beginning to think of returning to England, for he sought, and was granted, a general pardon by the English Parliament, 'at the special asking of the nobles, magnates and commonalty of the realm, and for good service rendered in the king's wars of France and elsewhere'. The pardon was granted on 2 March 1377, shortly before Edward III died and was succeeded by his ten year-old grandson, Richard II.[16]

Despite his request for a pardon, which would have eased his return to England, on 2 February 1377 he obeyed, however reluctantly, the papal legate's order to slaughter the people of Cesena

Sir John Hawkwood's Italy.

which, like Perugia and Bologna, had revolted against the Pope's authority. For whatever reason, Hawkwood and his men subsequently carried out, on behalf of the Pope, a ruthless massacre of the town's inhabitants that lasted three days. Eventually, perhaps sickened by the extent of this outrage, Hawkwood ordered a number of inhabitants to be spared. Despite his fearsome reputation, the Cesena massacre seems to be the only *crime* for which historians have ever held Hawkwood responsible.

Shortly after the destruction of Cesena, but before the anticipated arrival of a pardon from London, Hawkwood reached a turning point in his life. He shelved any plans for an immediate return to England and deserted to the Anti-Papal League. Perhaps in recognition of this move, on 3 May 1377, Bernabo Visconti gave Hawkwood his illegitimate daughter, Donnina, in marriage; one of several such daughters that he allied to the principal fighting men in his pay. Hawkwood was fifty-seven years old, earning perhaps 250,000 gold florins a year and approaching the peak of his military career. His marriage to Visconti's seventeen year-old daughter, his possession of castles and estates in Italy, together with his high income and considerable reputation as a successful mercenary, had made him at last an *Inglese italianato* whose future, however brief it might be, lay in Italy and not in England.

By the end of the summer Hawkwood was on the march once more and his soldiers drove the Pope's Breton army deep into the Sienese country-side. The threatened city of Siena sent a deputation to Hawkwood, as a result of which he attempted to make peace between the Pope and the Anti-Papal League. At the end of the campaign season that year he entered Florence where he was welcomed, although his peace proposals were rejected. In the spring of 1378, Hawkwood accompanied papal ambassadors to a meeting with Bernabo Visconti, but negotiations were aborted as a result of Gregory XI's death. It was left to Gregory's successor, Urban VI, to make peace, which he did without delay. In the same year Sir Edward de Berkeley and the poet Geoffrey Chaucer were sent from England in Richard II's name on a diplomatic mission to Lombardy. They were specifically instructed to meet Barnabo

Visconti and 'nostre cher et foial Johan Haukwoode' to discuss matters concerning the war against the Pope.[17] Clearly Hawkwood was a trusted, if unofficial, ambassador for Richard II when he met his countrymen at Bernabo's court in Milan in July 1378. It is possible that he had been persuaded not to return to England so that he could carry out these important duties at the court of the Viscontis, where he had both knowledge and influence.

Prior to Barnabo Visconti making peace with the Pope, Hawkwood had captured his old rival Sir John Thornbury, and doubtless it must have been with great satisfaction that he ransomed him. Shortly after his release Thornbury acquired a pardon similar to that granted to Hawkwood and he returned to England with his Italian wife and a great deal of money. Showing rather more business acumen than Hawkwood, he used the money that he had acquired in Italy to buy land and a manor in Little Munden, Hertfordshire. Later he became an MP and died in 1396 having outlived his rival by two years. Some sixty years later Thornbury's great-granddaughter, Philippa, married Hawkwood's great-grandson, Sir William Tyrell.[18]

In April 1378, Visconti sent Hawkwood and the German Lutz von Landau with an Anglo-German mercenary army to claim his wife's share of her family inheritance. The soldiers besieged Verona but, on payment of a huge sum in gold florins and the promise of an annual tribute, the Milanese army withdrew. In August of the same year Visconti ordered Hawkwood and Landau to return to Veronese territory. Their troops were utterly defeated by Hungarian mercenaries led by Stephan Laczsk and Visconti was forced to ask Verona for a truce. Hostilities recommenced in December when the Anglo-German army crossed the river Adige and advanced on Verona. Once again they were defeated by Laczsk's soldiers and forced to retreat to the Adige. Visconti took these defeats badly and withheld the pay of his *condottieri*. In response to this Hawkwood and Landau led their men in a *chevauchée*, first across the Bresciano then towards Cremona and finally into the countryside around Bologna. Enraged, Visconti put a price on their heads – just two years after his daughter had married Hawkwood.

Hawkwood and Landau decided to split up. Hawkwood remained inactive for a while, but he continued to receive a retainer from Florence and to march to the city's defence whenever it was threatened. Such was his reputation, that the mere threat of his presence was sometimes sufficient to deter even the most confident of his fellow *condottieri*, including rivals such as Alberigo de Barbiano, captain of the Compagnia di San Giorgio. In the autumn of 1378, Urban VI was challenged by a rival Pope who had been elected to an alternative papal throne as Clement VII. This was none other than Robert of Geneva, the papal legate who had ordered Hawkwood's destruction of Cesena. Urban VI continued to be recognised as Pope by England, but France supported his rival Clement VII.

During part of 1379, Hawkwood had his son-in-law Sir William Coggeshall (his daughter Antiocha's husband) with him in Italy. In a letter Hawkwood wrote to Lodovico Gonzaga on 3 March, he explained that Sir William had been in Milan for some time and now wished to go to Bagnacavallo with sixty horsemen for which he would need a safe conduct from Gonzaga.[19] It is likely that Coggeshall returned to England the same year in order to obtain seisin of his own inheritance in Essex, a legal process which was assisted by verbal evidence given to the escheator by Antiocha Coggeshall's uncle John Hawkwood the elder, and written evidence by Sir John himself.[20]

In 1380, Hawkwood received several large payments for his continued protection of Florence, and thereafter he remained in the city's service. In 1381 he sold, or mortgaged, his possessions in the Romagna because he was almost certainly in serious debt. Unlike some of his rivals (including Thornbury) Hawkwood's profession did not make him rich; partly perhaps, because he was scrupulous in paying the wages of his soldiers. During the same year the Peasants' Revolt took place in England and much damage was done to property in the neighbourhood of Sible Hedingham, possibly including that which belonged to his own family and his Coggeshall kin. It was at this time that Hawkwood and his growing family (daughters Giannetta, Caterina and Anna were born in 1378, 1379 and 1381

respectively) established a home in the vicinity of Florence (there is no record of the subsequent fate of the two sons of Hawkwood's presumed first marriage). It is probable that Hawkwood's five grandchildren by Antiocha Coggeshall were born at Great Codham Hall, Wethersfield, within a few years of the children of his second marriage.[21]

At the anti-French Pope's request in 1382, Hawkwood was temporarily released from his contract with Florence so that he could join Charles of Durazzo, who was fighting against Louis of Anjou for the crown of Naples. Hawkwood duly made his way to Naples, but the war soon ground to a halt as a result of inconclusive fighting and yet another outbreak of plague. Hawkwood again survived the contagion and returned to Tuscany, where he was secretly and successfully engaged by Florence to make war on Siena. Following this campaign he was able to purchase a number of estates, including the castle of Montecchio Vesponi which survives substantially as it was in Hawkwood's day. Early in 1385 Hawkwood, along with Sir Nicholas Dagworth and John Bacon, was appointed as an English ambassador to Naples, Florence and other Italian states, a clear indication of the esteem in which he was held in his own country. In June that year, Bernabo Visconti was violently deposed by his nephew Giangaleazzo Visconti, Count of Virtue, and later murdered. Hawkwood pragmatically agreed to serve Giangaleazzo (whose ultimate ambition was to overwhelm Florence) in return for an annual retainer.

In 1386, with the permission of the city of Florence, Hawkwood entered the service of Francesco Carrara, Marquis of Padua, who was then at war with Antonio della Scala of Verona. He took with him only a small personal following of mounted infantry and archers, some of them perhaps rather elderly veterans, and was given command of the Paduan army.

In January of the following year, Hawkwood made the now familiar crossing of the Adige at Castelbaldo and advanced unopposed into Veronese territory. As he approached the city of Verona he found that the enemy had laid waste to the countryside; his supply lines stretched to the limit, he had no choice but to retreat. On 11 March he reached Castagnaro on the bank of the

Adige. There he fought what was undoubtedly his most famous battle. Leading from the front, showing considerable physical courage and emulating the tactics of Crécy and Poitiers, Hawkwood and his smaller number of troops decisively defeated the Veronese army. Shortly after this victory Hawkwood returned to full-time service with Florence, but then began to dispose of his recently acquired estates, an indication that he was once more in debt, and almost certainly that Padua has not fully recompensed him for his services. In 1388, his son John, apparently the last of his children, was born to Donnina.

In 1390, when he could hardly have been less than seventy years of age, it is easy to imagine Hawkwood looking forward to retirement but, because he was still captain of war, he was again put in command of the Florentine army when conflict between Florence and Milan seemed imminent. In the campaign that followed, Hawkwood not only prevented an attack on Bologna by Jacopo dal Verme, but also utterly defeated his army in the field. In recognition of his outstanding services Florence increased Hawkwood's pension, provided dowries for his three daughters, and granted the freedom of the city to him and his son.

In order to support Hawkwood's efforts to protect the city, Florence hired the Count of Armagnac and his French mercenaries to invade Milanese territory from Provence. This was an ambitious plan, perhaps devised by Hawkwood, and it required that Armagnac should join forces with Hawkwood's army in a pincer movement designed to destroy the Milanese army as it advanced. Hawkwood crossed the Adige at Castelbaldo yet again and marched to within ten miles of Milan to wait for Armagnac. In this location, and before Armagnac could keep his rendezvous, Hawkwood was repeatedly attacked by a numerically superior force of Milanese troops. The Milanese avoided a pitched battle and were content to harass his army and attack his extended supply lines, much as the Veronese had done in 1387. As before, Hawkwood was obliged to conduct a fighting retreat through Castagnaro to the Adige; one that was brilliant in its execution. On the night of 11 July, against all odds, Hawkwood and the bulk of his forces were able to cross the river safely and withdraw to Castelbaldo. Despite Hawkwood's obvious defeat, the Milanese forces did not follow up their victory. Instead, only two weeks later, Jacopo dal Verme's army utterly destroyed Armagnac's forces at Alessandria and immediately invaded Tuscany. At this critically dangerous moment for Florence, Hawkwood took to the city's defence for the last time, and, with the forces he had saved on the Adige, he pushed dal Verme's troops back to Lucca and then into Liguria.

Hawkwood's gallant action enabled Florence to negotiate from a position of strength and make peace with Milan in 1392. This gave Hawkwood the leisure to consider solutions to his financial problems, to find husbands for his two older daughters and no doubt to think once more of returning to Essex. After a brief retirement however, he died in Florence, possibly of a stroke, during the night of 16/17 March 1394, shortly after the anniversary of his great victory at Castagnaro and at the age of seventy-four.

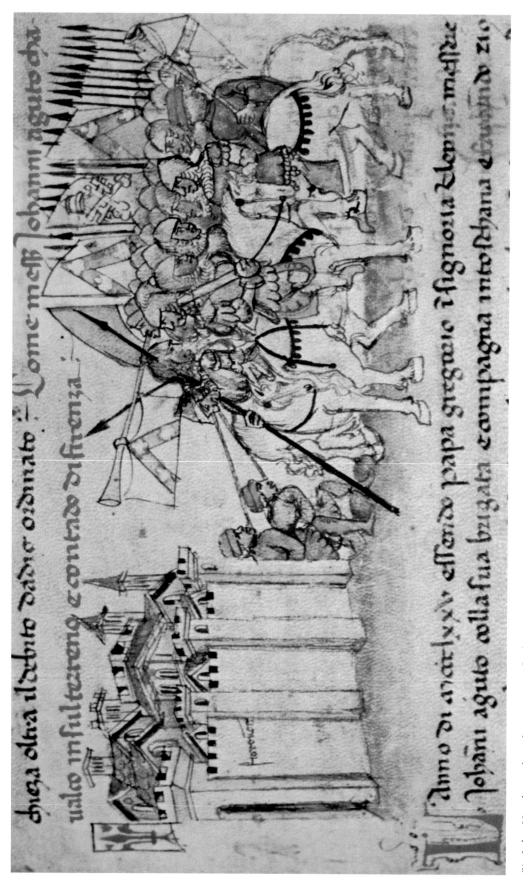

Sir John Hawkwood as the epitome of a brutal mercenary. Here depicted with his trumpeter Zuzzo, his personal bodyguard and papal soldiers at the gates of Florence. From the Chroniche del Sercambi *c.1400.*
© Archivo di Stato di Lucca.

Hawkwood's REPUTATION

At the height of his career Sir John Hawkwood was undoubtedly the most successful foreign *condottiere* anywhere in Italy. His reputation as an exceptional soldier is secure and rests not on the evidence of contemporary chronicles alone, but is supported by authentic historical documents such as correspondence. Perhaps, not surprisingly, his reputation in Italy is rather different from that in his own country, and Italians regard him as a despicable barbarian, the 'butcher of Cesena'. His very name, *Acuto*, is used to the present day to frighten unruly, young Italian children. Hawkwood's deeds must have appeared particularly cruel as contemporary Italians regarded anyone from northern Europe as a barbarian. In England, however, he is seen as a hero, a great fighting soldier and Englishman who effectively held the balance between the three principal Italian warring powers of the *Trecento*. His fellow countryman William Caxton referred to 'Syr Iohan Hawkwode … and many other whoos names shyne gloryously by their vertuous noblesse & actes that they did in thonour of thordre of chyvalry'.[22] Hawkwood's acquaintance and connections with so many of the leading figures in contemporary Italy gave him considerable influence. So too did his personal network formed through marriage, kinship, clientage and friendship.

Anyone who knows the Duomo in Florence is familiar with Uccello's painting of Sir John Hawkwood, and the picture does much to keep Hawkwood's memory alive. Probably the only contemporary representations of Hawkwood are in the *Chroniche del Sercambi* of *c.*1400 in the Archivio di Stato, Lucca.[23] Of the two, one shows Hawkwood, together with Zuzzo his trumpeter, at the head of his troops. After visiting Italy, the seventeenth-century Essex antiquary Richard Symonds recorded the following description of an early Hawkwood portrait which has long since disappeared:

In the Pallace of Medici upon Monte della Trinita in Rome … the Hall was hang[e]d w[i]th the Pictures of Illustrious men all over [th]e world & among them one w[i]th this fashioned Red Cap [he added a sketch of a man facing to the left wearing a hat] & these Words.
JOHANNES ACUTUS ANGL.[24]

These pictures are the only evidence we have of Hawkwood's physical appearance and there is no reason to think that they are actual portraits.

What then is the basis of Hawkwood's reputation? We know absolutely nothing of his supposed military service in France (we can only guess that he was present at some or all of Edward III's great victories), but it is clear that he gained his spurs in this conflict – literally and figuratively. His subsequent use of tactics that had been employed by the English at Crécy, Poitiers and elsewhere is perhaps an indication, but not evidence, that he was present at these battles. Parallels have been drawn for example, between these victories and the triumph of Hawkwood's Paduan forces over Verona at the Battle of Castagnaro in 1387.

In many ways Hawkwood retained his Englishness throughout his long career (some thirty-five years) as a foreign mercenary. However, first and foremost, Hawkwood was a great leader. He seems to have been a charismatic man who undoubtedly had many of the vital attributes of leadership: decisiveness; integrity; loyalty; imagination; and endurance. He was also an opportunist, a man who could, and did, turn disaster into triumph, and who was willing to gamble on the outcome of events in order to achieve success.

Hawkwood's effectiveness as a soldier owed much to his tactical skills. Despite his ferocity and ruthlessness, he was no mere brute. He was, in

Detail from Chroniques de France ou de St Denis *showing soldiers using scaling ladders in an attack on the walled city of Genoa.*

fact, the intellectual master of the battlefield; and his military failures were more often due to the inadequacy of his allies, than of his own planning and war-fighting ability. His masterly use of ground after careful reconnaissance (involving the collection and evaluation of intelligence) led to great victories. His skilful deployment of combined arms (armoured knights, infantry and artillery) confounded his opponents. As a general commanding, from time-to-time, the armies of Florence, Milan and the Pope, Hawkwood advised on, rather than determined, military strategy. Clearly, however, few statesmen would have been foolish enough to reject his advice. It was much to Hawkwood's credit that he did not use his military strength to establish himself as a local despot or ruler of a city, for it would certainly have been in his power to do so.

Hawkwood's English soldiers were known for their steadiness and discipline in battle, as well as their savagery in attack. Above all, their incomparable skill with the long bow was a battle-winning factor. Despite their prowess on the battlefield, the English were often uncontrollable when off duty and frequently indulged in rape and pillage when the opportunity arose. Unlike their Breton and Hungarian counterparts, however, the English were not known to be pathologically cruel; they did not kill for pleasure. The English (and in fourteenth-century Italy this term applied equally to Welsh, Scottish and Irish troops, as well as some other nationalities) were careful with their arms and equipment. These were always well maintained and it is said that the White Company got its name from the highly polished armour worn by its soldiers. Hawkwood's personal bodyguard and elite troops were invariably English, but he frequently employed Germans on his military campaigns; he and his men appear to have had an affinity with them.

Hawkwood was one of the first military leaders to use the term *lance* for reckoning numbers of troops. This was a fighting unit of three, and comprised two men-at-arms (one of whom may have been a knight), who carried a single very long lance between them, and a young page who looked after their horses. The pages were essential as men-at-arms rode into battle, then dismounted from their horses and fought on foot. Complementing the formations of lances were groups of archers, who when in battle were generally positioned on the flanks of the men-at-arms. Archers sometimes rode into battle and they uniformly employed the longbow (rather than the crossbow favoured by Italians and others), as well as other weapons such as swords and daggers. Their mission was to break up, and, if possible, disperse, oncoming enemy infantry and cavalry units and to engage enemy crossbowmen at long range before hand-to-hand fighting began.[25]

When in defence, Hawkwood's English troops were, like their successors in the eighteenth and nineteenth centuries, invariably steady and controlled enough to await, then overwhelm the onslaught of their enemies with the intention of destroying them by their superior fire power. Many English mercenaries also carried as standard equipment short lengths of scaling ladder that could be lashed together immediately before an attack on town walls. Although he only made limited use of guns, Hawkwood was one of the first medieval generals successfully to deploy field artillery.

Another characteristic Hawkwood tactic was the night attack, or attack at first light, usually after a forced march over a long distance and at considerable speed. Such audacious night attacks often caught his enemies unawares and were essentially an early form of *Blitzkrieg*. Their habitual tolerance of cold and rain enabled English soldiers to campaign until late in the year, something their enemies were generally reluctant to do.

As has been said, when preparing for war, Hawkwood relied heavily on intelligence regarding enemy strength and intentions. He engaged spies to gather military intelligence, and he is also known to have received advice from fortune-tellers on this subject. A surviving contemporary copy of a letter addressed to Hawkwood *c.*1390 purports to foretell the outcome of conflict in Italy by means of 'astronomy'.[26] Hawkwood was also skilled in the use of deception and camouflage to mask his military operations. For example, on at least one

Copy of a letter dated c.1390 addressed to Sir John Hawkwood purporting to foretell the outcome of a conflict in Italy by means of Lastronomie. Reproduced by kind permission of the Marquess of Bath, Longleat House, Warminster, Wiltshire. Longleat MS (North Muniment Room) 370.

occasion when tactically withdrawing from the enemy, he left trumpeters to sound calls and campfires to burn long after his troops had decamped during the night.

A powerful contributory factor to Hawkwood's success was his personal loyalty and integrity. Unusually for a man in his profession, he kept his word and fulfilled the terms of each *condotta* (contract) he signed. It seems that he paid his troops before taking his own share and thereby ensured their loyalty to him. He also impoverished himself in the process, and eventually sank deep into debt from which he never fully recovered. It is also said that each *condotta* he signed contained a clause that specified his refusal to act against English interests in any circumstances, an indication of his own loyalty to the English Crown.

Hawkwood could remain loyal beyond good sense and reason, as he did with the Pope. Long after it would have been sensible to terminate his contract due to the non-payment of fees, he continued to fight on the Pope's behalf. It was only after the shameful massacre at Cesena that Hawkwood felt compelled to desert his papal employer. Hawkwood's loyalty is also apparent from the lengths to which he went in order to support his family and friends. For example, in May 1378 the Council of Ten offered Hawkwood a large sum of money to ravage Paduan territory, but he declined on the grounds of his friendship with its lord.

In financial terms Hawkwood's life could be judged to have been less than successful. He did, after all, die an impoverished old man far from the homeland where he wanted to end his days. But what a life he had led! There had been so many great victories and comparatively few defeats. He had earned respect amounting almost to adulation from the citizens of Florence whose city he and his soldiers had successfully protected for more than twenty years. As early as 1377 when he obtained a pardon from Richard II, Hawkwood was famous and well respected in his own country. The *Polychronicon* of Ralph Higden, written in England during Hawkwood's lifetime, refers to him as '*miles famosus*'.[27]

We know that Hawkwood married at least once, and that he had five sons and five daughters by several different women, including his wife Donnina. The mother, or mothers, of Hawkwood's older children are not known and it is not clear whether he was married before he met Donnina. He also acknowledged a bastard son, John, who was destined to be a priest. Despite this comparatively large family, Hawkwood's descendants died out in the male line within some fifteen years of his death. In the female line, particularly through his daughter Antiocha, many of his descendants are with us today. As to his possessions, he sold most of what he had in Italy to pay his huge local debts, but he did leave some of his English estates to his wife and son, John junior. What happened to this property after their deaths is a matter of conjecture.

Hawkwood was a good soldier. He appears to have risen through the ranks, was knighted, and became captain-general of the Florentine army by his own efforts. After a shaky start he became the ultimate professional mercenary. He was immensely competitive in the world of mercenaries, securing contracts for himself and his men against fierce opposition. He was a businessman and his business was war. He was also a diplomat, employed not only by his king and countrymen to represent English interests in Italy, but also by a succession of Italian cities to act as a power-broker and to negotiate on their behalf in peace and in war. He seems also to have got on well with a varied succession of employers, as well as the soldiers of many nationalities who fought in his service.

By the standards of his time he was not a particularly cruel man and used no more force than was necessary to achieve victory for his employers. However, his personal responsibility for the massacre at Cesena would certainly amount to a war crime today. It was perhaps only on this occasion that he deserved the epithet: *Inglese italianato, è un diavolo incarnato* – the Italianate Englishman is a devil incarnate.[28]

Was Hawkwood simply the brutal medieval warrior depicted in the *Chroniche del Sercambi* manuscript or the statesman-like field commander and Renaissance man portrayed by Uccello? It would be fair to say that he began as one and finished as the other.

Sible Hedingham village sign depicting local hero Sir John Hawkwood.   Photograph Clare Banks

Hawkwood's ESSEX

Medieval Essex was the surviving heartland of a large territory which, before it was partitioned in the late Saxon period as Essex, Middlesex, Surrey and Hertfordshire, was the kingdom of the East Saxons. The boundaries of early medieval Essex were defined by the rivers Stour, Lea, Stort and Thames, together with the North Sea, and encompassed an area of about a million acres. Despite these clearly defined boundaries, much of the countryside of Essex was virtually indistinguishable from the borderlands of Suffolk, Kent, Hertfordshire and Cambridgeshire, which formed with Essex a number of pays or continuous landscapes. These landscapes occurred not only in geographical, but also in political and social terms, so that there were strong connections of kinship and friendship between the gentry on both sides of the county border.

At the time of Sir John Hawkwood's birth (*c*.1320), there were some four hundred villages in Essex, many of them with scattered outlying hamlets. Where a village nucleus existed, it was often in the vicinity of the principal manor house or hall and its adjacent parish church. The church/hall complex is an enduring feature of the Essex countryside and is still to be found in the majority of Essex villages. Unlike the rest of East Anglia, the total number of villages in Essex hardly fluctuated as a result of the fourteenth century's demographic disasters of famine and plague; few Essex villages were entirely deserted in this period.

The large open fields often associated with the manorial system were comparatively rare in medieval Essex, although some were to be found in the north-west of the county; most Essex manors tended to have numerous, relatively small, enclosed fields. Many of these ancient closes still survive but, as Oliver Rackham has observed, it is probably by visiting Essex woodland and marshland that we can get closest to seeing the late medieval countryside.[29] Essex manor houses and churches with substantial fourteenth-century features are still in existence and they provide evidence for the lifestyle of Hawkwood's family and their contemporaries.

In the early fourteenth century there were approximately fourteen hundred manors in Essex, most of them with an individual manor house. The large number of manors and petty lords at this time mean that it is probable that lordship was weak at local level, particularly when manorial demesnes were beginning to be leased out to peasants who paid rent rather than gave labour service to their lord. It was characteristic of Essex in the late medieval period that many manor houses were moated (more than seven hundred moats have been identified), and that deer parks (over a hundred) were widely distributed across the county. By 1350, there were some four hundred parish churches, half of which survive to the present day as substantially medieval buildings; others remain, but have been rebuilt.[30] There were also at least seventy freestanding chapels (mainly associated with manor houses) and some fifty religious houses, including abbeys and priories. The majority of these chapels and religious houses have been destroyed almost without trace.

In general terms the medieval Essex gentry were the landowners who took their place between the higher nobility (the peerage) and the richest peasants (the sub-gentry) in the hierarchy of the county community. The gentry may also be defined as those individuals who generally held one or more manors, but more accurately as those who were actually recognised as gentry by the rest of the community in which they lived.

By the early 1300s, the Essex gentry had evolved from what in the previous two centuries had been simply a group of knights resident in the

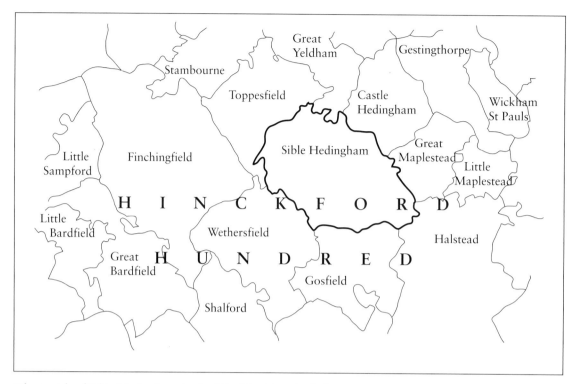

The parish of Sible Hedingham in the Hinckford hundred, Essex.

county to a feudal hierarchy headed by a small number of rich knights, but largely consisting of a new group of lesser landowners who had gradually become known as 'esquires'. In 1322, a list of high-ranking fighting men compiled for Parliament showed those in Essex who were capable of fighting in the king's wars comprised twelve bannerets (senior knights), forty-four knights and eighty-one esquires.[31] Within a century of Hawkwood's birth the knights and esquires were joined by another group known as 'gentlemen' (mainly the relatively low income owners of a single small manor), who had emerged amongst the gentry and whose status was recognised by statute in 1413.[32]

By the late fourteenth century an elite group, subordinate only to the king and the higher nobility and consisting of rich knights and esquires, had formed within the Essex gentry. We now recognise them as the principal or regional gentry. Although usually resident in the county, their interests were not exclusively in Essex as many of them also held land in neighbouring counties; this gave them a wider, often regional, focus. Not only were they the richest men outside the higher nobility of Essex, but as a group they

had a virtual monopoly of the most important county offices including those of sheriff, knight of the shire (MP), justice of the peace and escheator. Below them in the social hierarchy were a group that could be termed the greater, or county, gentry, whose landed interests lay mainly in Essex. The third, and by far the largest group comprised the lesser or parish gentry whose horizons rarely extended beyond the village in which they held their single manor. Immediately beneath the gentry in the social order of the time was a large underclass of rich peasants, comprising those described as 'yeomen' or 'husbandmen', some of whom were eventually able to acquire sufficient land and 'worship' to attain gentry status. By c.1420, the medieval Essex gentry had reached its final development; the regional gentry were knights, the county gentry were esquires, and the parish gentry were gentlemen.

What distinguished the Essex gentry from those of many other counties in the later fourteenth century was the exceptionally dynamic nature of the society in which they lived and the comparative ease with which this society could be entered. Upward mobility was constant; as gentry families died out in the male line, lesser families moved up and took their places (often literally) either by purchase or by marriage to eligible heiresses. It was the golden age of the parvenu; humble origins were no bar to a man who acquired (by whatever means) sufficient money to buy his way into a society which, however reluctantly, recognised worship and manorial lordship, rather than gentle birth, as the criteria for gentry status. Had Hawkwood returned from Italy at the height of his success, he would undoubtedly have been accepted as one of the county elite despite his minor gentry origins. This was certainly the case for Sir John Thornbury when he abandoned his career as a *condottiere* and returned to England to live in Hertfordshire as a country gentleman.[33]

The evidence of tax returns and records of a buoyant land market which precipitated the constant inflow of upwardly mobile individuals from the north and west of England, (and occasionally from Wales and Ireland), indicates that Essex was a wealthy, dynamic county in the fourteenth century.[34] No doubt the county's proximity to London was part of the attraction, but Essex also represented an excellent investment opportunity in terms of land and productivity. The gentry were widely dispersed, but the richer families tended to avoid the Essex coast and the densely wooded areas in the south-west of the county. Instead they favoured the more attractive (and productive) manors in the fertile valleys of Essex's north, west and central areas.

By about 1300, medieval Essex had reached its apogee in terms of population and land clearance. Wheat and barley were the principal crops but other cereals were also grown; the majority of agricultural land consisted of London clay or

boulder clay, and a plough team could comprise as many as four horses and four oxen in order to work the heaviest land. Woodland was intensely managed, mainly by coppicing but also by pollarding. Dairying (cattle and sheep) and pig rearing were vital components of the rural economy and Essex became proverbially productive in respect of hard, long-lasting cheese (made from sheep's milk) and bacon.[35]

The principal non-agricultural industry in Essex in Hawkwood's time was cloth-making from locally produced low-grade wool. Much of this activity was concentrated in the Hinckford hundred, and poll tax returns show that the village of Sible Hedingham had a large number of cloth-workers in its population.[36] Some of the cloth was exported to Italy, notably to Florence, and this may perhaps have given rise to stories that Hawkwood had been apprenticed to a tailor. Other industries in late medieval Essex were fishing (including oysters), and the production of salt, cutlery, pottery, tiles, bricks, hides and wool. There were at least eighty markets at this time and fifteen chartered boroughs; useful measures of the county's prosperity.[37] The Hinckford hundred (containing Sible Hedingham) was the third richest area in Essex in 1327 and comprised fifty-two parishes.[38]

At the beginning of the fourteenth century, life expectancy in England for men and women was little more than forty years and few people would have lived to see their grandchildren grow beyond early childhood. The population of Essex was about 130,000 in 1320, but successive episodes of famine and plague during the fourteenth century, including the Black Death in 1348-9, reduced it to about 65,000, the approximate level it had been at the time of the Domesday survey in 1086.[39]

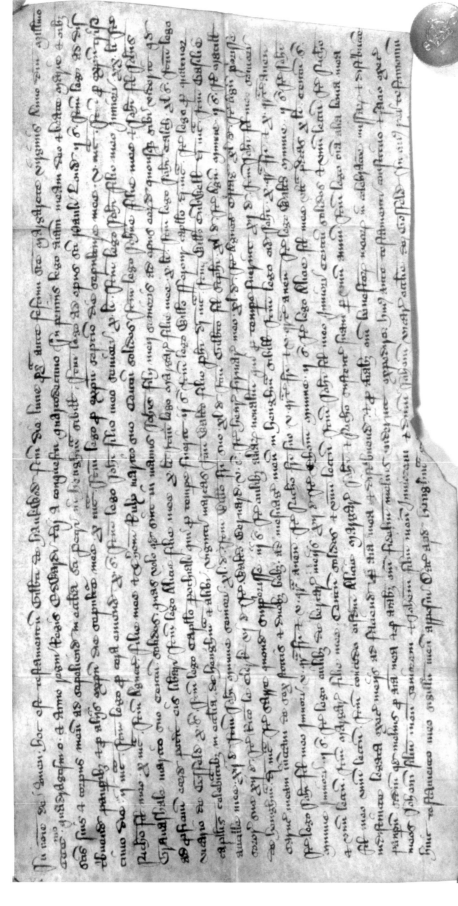

Will of Gilbert de Hawkwood of Sible Hedingham dated 18 July 1340. In it he leaves 'my son John junior' bequests of grain, cash, a bed and his keep for a year.

Hawkwood's ORIGINS

As to the origin of the Hawkwood family there can be little certainty. Possibly it took its name from Hawks Wood in Gosfield, a small but ancient wood close to the present Hawkwood Farm. The 'hawk' element of this place-name has nothing to do with birds, but rather from the Middle English word *halke* meaning a 'nook' or 'corner'. Whatever their origin, the earliest recorded Hawkwoods were villeins and therefore of unfree status. A cartulary relating to the Essex land held by the Knights of St John of Jerusalem contains several records of thirteenth-century Hawkwoods who were probably Sir John Hawkwood's ancestors. The earliest of these references is to the sale by Robert de Hasting to Simon de Odewell (of Odewell's manor, Gestingthorpe) of property including Alexander de Hawkwood, his family and their labour services; they were sold *c.*1231.[40]

In about 1248 Walter de Hawkwood (possibly the son of Alexander), whilst in the service of Geoffrey de Liston (*d.*1267), whose manor of Liston Hall adjoins Hawkwood Farm in Gosfield, was called on to witness a grant made by Walter the Carpenter who lived in Sible Hedingham.[41] The Hawkwood/Liston connection was to recur in later generations and may account for the rise of the Hawkwood family. The Listons of Liston (near Sudbury) were knights in the thirteenth and fourteenth centuries and the Hawkwoods perhaps acquired land and other property through service with them.

Two or three generations after Walter de Hawkwood, when the list of taxpayers for the lay subsidy of 1319/20 was drawn up, there were three Hawkwoods assessed for tax in Sible Hedingham. William paid 4*s*. 1¼*d*.; Philip paid 1*s*. 2¾*d*.; and Ellen (probably a widow) paid 1*s*. 2¾*d*.[42] Clearly

Hawkwood's Farm, Gosfield. A building on this site was the home of Sir John Hawkwood's brother, John Hawkwood the elder.
Photograph Christopher Starr

Hawkwood Manor, Sible Hedingham, stands on the site of a house which may have been Sir John Hawkwood's birthplace.

Photograph Clare Banks

the Hawkwoods had risen a little in importance and their liability for tax suggests that they may no longer have been unfree, although the richer villeins did pay taxes. All three taxpayers may have been dead by 1327, as they are not listed in the returns for the tax levied on moveable property that year.[43]

It appears that the heir to the early Hawkwoods of Sible Hedingham was Gilbert Hawkwood (who like Walter usually described himself as 'de' Hawkwood). He first appears in 1314/15 as a feoffee for his son-in-law John Graveshall, the head of a family that had held the manor of Graveshall in Sible Hedingham from the earls of Oxford, since the time when the Hawkwoods had been but villeins.[44] In 1317, Gilbert witnessed a grant of land from Geoffrey Shorthose to John the Potter who, like Gilbert, lived in Potter Street, Sible Hedingham.[45]

Gilbert de Hawkwood is invariably described as a tanner, but there is neither evidence nor much likelihood that he followed this unsavoury occupation. If he did have a connection with a tannery it is probable that he was its owner, for he was a man of substance in the villages of Gosfield, Finchingfield and Sible Hedingham; he was certainly of higher social status than a tanner. During Gilbert's lifetime Sible Hedingham was in the centre of the Essex cloth-working area, so it is perhaps more likely that he had some connection with this industry rather than with tanning. Undoubtedly, many of his acquaintances and neighbours would have been involved in cloth-making and their children would have grown up with the Hawkwood children.

As has been said, Gilbert de Hawkwood was probably the descendant of a succession of Hawkwoods in the Sible Hedingham/Gosfield area who had accrued sufficient wealth to acquire and sustain their freedom. Gilbert eventually moved much further up the social scale and achieved parish gentry status through the possession of manorial land acquired, perhaps, by marriage or by service to an established member of the gentry. In 1324, he stood surety for Sir John de Liston (*d*.1332), a tenant of the Earl of Oxford, at his election as Knight of the Shire for Essex, an indication both of Gilbert's wealth and local standing.[46] It is possible that Gilbert may have served as steward or in some other administrative capacity for the Liston family or for the earls of Oxford.

When assessed for the tax on moveable property of 1327, only six inhabitants out of the forty-four listed as of Sible Hedingham were required to pay more than Gilbert de Hawkwood. His assessment in the nearby village of Finchingfield was proportionally high. For reasons that are not clear he was taxed there but not in Gosfield where he also held land.[47] A year later Gilbert de Hawkwood sued one Hugh de Kingsdon for debt, and in 1336 he and his son-in-law John de Graveshall witnessed a grant on behalf of the Rector of Bradwell-on-Sea.[48]

Another indication of Gilbert's wealth is that he planned to dispose of a total of more than one hundred pounds through bequests in his will (although it is possible that he was giving away what he did not have).[49] He left his eldest son John ten pounds and 'my yoke of six stots and two oxen [the boulder clay he farmed must have been very heavy to require such a strong team of draught animals], at my messuage in Sible Hedingham' together with ten quarters of wheat and ten of oats. The 'messuage' to which he refers was undoubtedly the present-day Hawkwood Manor in Swan Street (formerly Potter Street). This was first referred to as a manor in 1449, but it is quite possible that it operated as one long before that date as it was not unusual for manors to be described as messuages.[50]

Although his will is in the British Library, Gilbert de Hawkwood's testament has not survived. We do not know how he disposed of his land or indeed what it consisted of, but it appears that the bulk of the Hawkwood patrimony passed to Gilbert's eldest son. Unlike his forbears who were buried in the churchyard with nothing to mark their graves, Gilbert specified in his will that he was to be buried inside the church, thus anticipating by many years his son's high status memorial in the same building. ▨

King Richard II who requested the return of Sir John Hawkwood's remains from Florence to England in 1395.

National Portrait Gallery, London

Hawkwood's FAMILY

The extent of the inner circle of the Hawkwood family of Sible Hedingham is known from Gilbert de Hawkwood's will of 1340. There were three sons: John the elder, John the younger and Nicholas, and four daughters: Agnes (married to Thomas Ruly), Joan (married to John Graveshall), Alice and Margaret (both unmarried in 1340).[51]

The Munne family of Sible Hedingham was closely connected with the Hawkwoods, and no less than seven of them are named in Gilbert's will. A possible explanation is that the Munnes were his wife's family and that the John Munne, taxed at eighteen pence in 1327, was Gilbert's father-in-law.[52] Perhaps John Munne was godfather to one or both of Gilbert's two sons of the same name.

The elder of Gilbert's two sons named John was born *c.*1315 and on Gilbert's death inherited his father's land. No record remains of the document or documents that transferred the patrimony to John the elder, but it was probably done by means either of a testament or deed of enfeoffment. The latter process is more likely as, in 1344, four messuages and land in Gosfield, Sible Hedingham and Bocking were transferred from John Galant (Vicar of Gosfield and one of Gilbert's executors) and John Calch (a beneficiary under Gilbert's will), both of whom were acting as feoffees, to John the elder, his wife Margery (or Margaret) and their young son John (represented by a lawyer named William Cockerell) by means of a fine sued out in the Court of Common Pleas.[53] It is possible too, that three of the messuages listed in the fine were actually the manors of Gosfield Hall and Park Hall, in Gosfield, and Hawkwoods in Sible Hedingham (which is not otherwise referred to as a manor until 1449).[54] The fourth messuage referred to in the 1344 transaction may have been the property in Gosfield now known as Hawkwood's Farm which probably never had manorial status.

John Hawkwood the elder of Sible Hedingham, who must for much of his life have been overshadowed by the exploits of his famous younger brother, was a man of substance in his own right, although he never achieved more than local importance.[55] In the light of his subsequent career he appears to have been a long-term member of the household of the earls of Oxford at Hedingham, possibly as steward. Having inherited the Hawkwood family patrimony in 1340, John the elder may have continued to farm it as his father had done, growing cereal crops and running flocks of sheep. By 1348, shortly before the outbreak of the Black Death, he was sufficiently well-to-do that he obtained a royal licence to exempt him from the burdens of public office to which he would otherwise have been subject on account of his wealth and status.[56] This licence excused him from being put on 'assizes, juries or recognitions, and from being made mayor, sheriff, coroner, escheator or other bailiff or minister of the king, against his will'. He had the licence confirmed in 1378 at the cost of half a mark which he paid to the King.[57]

In 1358, John the elder had in wardship Gilbert Cole (possibly Gilbert de Hawkwood's godson) of Sible Hedingham and in 1363 witnessed a deed for John French of Halstead as 'domino Johanne de Hawkwood'.[58] His domicile in Gosfield during this period is confirmed by a deed of 1372, in which he is described as 'of Gosfield'.[59] It was part of the endowment of the convent at Castle Hedingham founded by Alberic de Vere, first Earl of Oxford. The prioress had the advowson of Gosfield church and in view of Gilbert de Hawkwood's other known connections with the nunnery, he may have been her man of business.

The inquisition post mortem of Thomas de Vere, Earl of Oxford, who died in 1371, shows that not only did John the elder hold two-thirds of a knight's fee from the Earl in Sible

Hedingham, but also that he was sufficiently valued and trusted as a retainer to have been appointed the Earl's executor. For his services in this capacity he received a bequest of twenty marks out of the Earl's estate.[60] John the elder also acted as the Earl's feoffee for land in Leicestershire, Rutland and Kent; he later served as feoffee for Countess Maud, the Earl's widow.[61] A further indication of John the elder's status was the grant, in 1376, of a papal indult that permitted him the considerable privilege of choosing his own confessor and having a portable altar in his house.[62]

In old age John Hawkwood the elder continued to accumulate land and a fine of 1378 shows that Thomas Tewe, the Earl of Oxford's park and warren keeper and esquire in the Earl's household, sold land and six bondsmen to John the elder, a distant echo of the sale of Alexander Hawkwood and his family a hundred and fifty years before.[63] In 1379, John the elder had sufficient capital to lend Richard II twenty pounds with which to help fund the war in France; he was one of only a small number of Essex gentry who lent the King money on this occasion.[64] In 1380, Sir John Hawkwood demonstrated his trust in his older brother by appointing him his feoffee, possibly forty years after their last meeting.[65] A rental preserved in the Essex Record Office shows that John the elder held small amounts of land in Gosfield and Sible Hedingham from Colne Priory c.1380.[66]

In the poll tax returns of 1381, John Hawkwood the elder and his wife Margaret (this may have been the same woman to whom he was married in 1344, or he may have remarried) were together assessed at five shillings.[67] Hawkwood's degree or status is referred to in the margin of the return as 'frankeleyn' a term implying wealth, minor gentry status and local importance (Chaucer's Franklin had been sheriff and knight of the shire), but someone in fact who might still be only a generation or two removed from the peasantry. It is not known when John the elder died, but he is last mentioned in a rental of Graves Hall, Sible Hedingham dated 1385.[68] In 1397 the lawyer Robert Rikedon of Witham, who had previously acted as a trustee for Sir John Hawkwood, founded a chantry in Witham

church for John Hawkwood the elder and his wife Margaret.[69] The fate of their son John is unknown; in 1368 he was a witness to a grant of land in Kelvedon by Henry Prat, but is not heard of again.[70]

In addition to his chantry at Witham church, John Hawkwood the elder may be commemorated by one of the late medieval graveslabs in the floor of Gosfield church. A more tangible link with Sir John's elder brother is a fine seal impression on a document of 1341 in the National Archives which shows John the elder's coat of arms: a lion rampant, within a cusped quatrefoil.[71] The inscription on the seal impression reads: *Secretum Iohannis de Haukwode*. During his long life John the elder clearly rose above the social status into which he was born.

We know very little of Hawkwood's younger brother Nicholas. He was in holy orders and in 1363 held court at the manor of Park Hall, Gosfield on behalf of his brother John the elder.[72] In the same year, as 'a poor priest of the diocese of London' he petitioned the Pope for a benefice in the gift of the prior and convent of Stoke by Clare in Suffolk.[73] It is not recorded whether his petition was successful.

Of Sir John Hawkwood's sisters we know that Agnes, the first named in her father's will and presumably the eldest, was the wife of Thomas Ruly in 1340. She was left a modest bequest of £5 by her father, as was her married sister, Joan. Curiously, the sums were not to be paid at once, but were to remain in the hands of their elder brother John 'for their need, and to be paid to them as he considers it for their advantage'. Nothing is known of Hawkwood's younger sisters Alice and Margaret (unmarried in 1340), other than their father's bequest of £10 to each of them.[74]

The Ruly family were local minor gentry of similar, but more ancient, status than the Hawkwoods. They first appear in a deed of c.1180-90 in which Robert de Roilia witnessed a grant of land to the Hospitallers in Sturmer.[75] Subsequently, the family became widely distributed in Essex, but it was centred at Ramsey in the north-east of the county where it held the manor of (Le) Ray from the earls of Oxford. Morant says that the first Ruly in Ramsey was William Ruly and that his descendants did homage for the manor of Ray (it being half a knight's fee) in 1291. Morant, who had probably seen it, wrote that the 'mansion house is about a mile, north north-east from the Church. Here was formerly a Chapel, dedicated to St. Peter'. Ray Farm now represents this house though, according to Morant, it was known as Rulyes in the reign of Henry VI after it had passed from the Ruly family.[76]

The *Essex Fines* show three generations of the Ruly family active in Ramsey: William Ruly in 1254 and two Geoffrey Rulys between 1316 and 1362.[77] The Aid list of 1346 confirms that there were at least two Geoffrey Rulys - father and son.[78] In 1303, the father held a quarter of a knight's fee in the manor of Ramsey from the Earl of Oxford together with Thomas de Lavenham, and the son held the same fee in 1346 with Richard de la Pantrie.[79] In 1428, the Aid list records simply that this fee was held by the successor of Geoffrey Ruly, the family presumably having died out in the male line in Ramsey.[80] A Hubert Ruly, who had formerly, according to the Aid of 1303, held land in nearby Bradfield, was doubtless a kinsman of the Rulys of Ramsey.[81]

The branch of the Ruly family that was closest geographically to the Hawkwoods of Sible Hedingham lived in Finchingfield where Richard Ruly (dead by 1279) held land. Richard's widow Sabina, son Thomas and daughter Margaret were living in 1279 when Margaret sued out a fine relating to land in Finchingfield.[82] Her son Thomas may have been the ancestor of the Thomas Ruly (whose origins are otherwise unknown) who married Gilbert de Hawkwood's daughter Agnes, both of whom were living in 1340.

It seems that Agnes Ruly remarried after her husband's death for, in 1346, John Kemp and his wife Agnes held half a knight's fee in Finchingfield that had formerly belonged to Thomas Ruly.[83] This is unlikely to have been the Thomas Ruly who was alive in 1279, but it is possibly a descendant and namesake, and this would establish Agnes Hawkwood's first husband

as a member of the Finchingfield Ruly clan. John Kemp of Spain's Hall (his father Nicholas having married the heiress Margaret de Ispagnia) was a rising man, who appears in the Court of Common Pleas records between 1343 and 1366 as an attorney. By 1383 he had remarried, his second wife being Katherine with whom he later purchased land in Finchingfield.[84] In 1375 the same John Kemp had enfeoffed John Hawkwood the elder – who was probably his first wife's brother – with land in Finchingfield, Great Sampford and Great Bardfield.[85] John Kemp's descendants (perhaps by his first wife Agnes Hawkwood) lived at Spain's Hall, Finchingfield until the death of the last John Kemp in 1727.

Joan, Gilbert de Hawkwood's second daughter, is described in his will as being the wife of John, son of John Graveshall. By a fine sued out in 1314/15, John de Graveshall [senior] and his wife Agnes, probably the parents of Gilbert Hawkwood's son-in-law, acquired a messuage and more than four hundred acres in Sible Hedingham from Master Richard de Canfield and Gilbert de Hawkwood.[86] This messuage was undoubtedly Graveshall's manor in Sible Hedingham and the fine effected a transfer of the property from Richard de Canfield and Gilbert Hawkwood acting as feoffees to John de Graveshall [junior] his deceased father's heir. The manor is now known as Grave's Hall and lies north-west of the church; the present house is modern and is adjacent to a caravan park. However, the manor's ancient name is preserved in nearby Grassall's Wood. It seems that Joan Hawkwood married the son of John [senior] and Agnes Graveshall, and that the parents were still alive in 1337 when they sued out a fine regarding the purchase of one hundred and sixty-two acres in Sible Hedingham.[87]

The Graveshall family had held land in Sible Hedingham from the earls of Oxford since at least the reign of Henry I and were of higher status than either the Hawkwoods or the Rulys. A Colne Priory cartulary records a series of gifts to the Priory made by the de Vere family and many of these involve the Graveshall (or Grossvassal) family.[88] The earliest such reference is dated 1111 and is a confirmation by Henry I of gifts to Colne Priory made by Aubrey de Vere, including a grant of one third of the tithe of

William Grossvassal. There is a similar confirmation by Ralph d'Escures, Archbishop of Canterbury, of gifts to the monks of Colne between 1114 and 1122, including one-third of the tithe of William Grossvassal, and another gift made c.1135 of the same tithe by Aubrey de Vere. There are also confirmations of grants dated c.1148-62, including one of a third of the tithe of Warin Grossvassal, William's successor, to Colne Priory. Morant cites Godfrey Grossvassal as having held the manor of Graveshall from Aubrey de Vere, first Earl of Oxford who died in 1194.[89] Adam de Gravassall (who purchased twenty-eight acres of land in Sible Hedingham in 1253/54) and his brother John witnessed a number of documents locally between c.1262 and c.1265, in one case with Walter de Hawkwood (possibly the father or grandfather of Gilbert de Hawkwood).[90] The John Graveshall and his wife Maud who are mentioned in a fine of 1284/85 were probably the parents of John Graveshall fl.1314/15.[91] Gilbert de Hawkwood's son-in-law, John Graveshall, held the manor of Graves Hall from the de Vere family as a knight's fee in 1361 on the death of the seventh Earl of Oxford, and in 1371 on the death of the eighth Earl.[92]

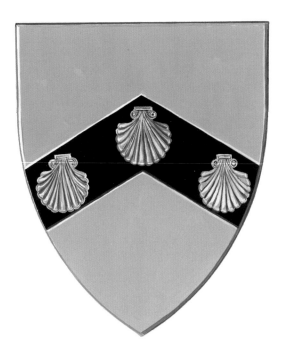

The arms of Sir John Hawkwood: argent, a chevron sable, with three scallops argent thereon. The scallops (or cockleshells) appear to have been adopted in deference to Hawkwood's son-in-law Sir William Coggeshall of Wethersfield, whose arms included four scallops.

Painted by Ann Bowen, Painter-Stainers' Company, London (2006)

CHAPTER SIX

Hawkwood's NETWORK

During his military service in France, Sir John Hawkwood is likely to have made contact with a number of the gentry and ordinary soldiers from his native county. Serving in the former group was Sir John Gildesburgh of Wennington, who fought at the Battles of Crécy and Poitiers, and was later a prominent member of parliament (he was Speaker in 1380). He was connected with the brothers Sir Henry and Thomas Coggeshall (father and uncle respectively of Hawkwood's son-in-law Sir William). There was also Sir Robert Marney of Layer Marney; he too fought at Crécy and Poitiers. Another Essex knight who almost certainly knew Hawkwood in France was Sir Robert Swinborne of Little Horkesley. We do not know how or when Hawkwood rose from the ranks to a position of command in the war with France, in fact we cannot be entirely sure that he did. It is probable, however, that he commanded a company, and that his knighthood was a reward for his military services. It is not known who knighted Hawkwood or when, but his entitlement to this honour was certainly recognised by Edward III who addressed him in correspondence as Sir John.[93] Once he had attained the rank of knight, this son of a minor member of the Essex gentry would have been on equal terms with the long-established county elite who, it seems, had no reservations in accepting parvenus with the right credentials.

It was probably through his well-connected son-in-law Sir William Coggeshall that Sir John would have made his wider contacts with the Essex gentry. Sir William was born on 20 July 1358 (as his proof of age inquest on 26 July 1379 established) and inherited ten manors from his father Sir Henry Coggeshall on the latter's death in 1375 - eventually providing him with an annual income of at least one hundred and fifty pounds, one of the highest landed incomes in Essex at the time.[94] In March 1379, whilst still the ward of his uncle, Thomas Coggeshall, he was soldiering in Italy as a *condottiere* and by that date had married Hawkwood's daughter Antiocha.[95] It may have been Thomas Coggeshall or John, Lord Bourchier, another of his uncles, who encouraged Sir William's military ambitions. On 30 July 1379, following the proof of age inquest, Roger Ketterich the escheator for Essex and Hertfordshire, was ordered to give seisin of his patrimony to Sir William despite his absence abroad. Sir William had proved his age before the escheator, and in doing so had arranged supporting documentation in the form of 'the petition of John Haukewode, witnessing by letters that the said William is over sea in his company'.[96] In the light of this information Richard II had remitted Sir William's homage and fealty until his return to England. Having met and married Hawkwood's daughter, apparently whilst serving with Sir John, Sir William Coggeshall returned to Essex *c.*1380 (he does not appear in the 1381 poll tax returns). His wife Antiocha was living at Gosfield with her uncle and aunt at the time of the taxation.[97] It seems that Sir William was knighted overseas, possibly by his father-in-law. Sir John Hawkwood may have known not only Sir William's father Sir Henry, but also his grandfather Sir John Coggeshall (who died in 1361), as the Coggeshall's capital manor was Great Codham Hall, Wethersfield, a short distance from Sible Hedingham.

Upon his return to Essex, Sir William would have been in a position to promote or defend his father-in-law's interests for he was soon an active member of Countess Joan de Bohun's circle of affinity. This included Walter, Lord Fitzwalter (*d.*1386) and prominent members of the Essex gentry including Sir Alexander Walden, Sir William Berland, Sir William Marney and Sir Robert Tey. There would also have been a connection with Countess Joan's brothers, Bishop Arundel and Richard, Earl of

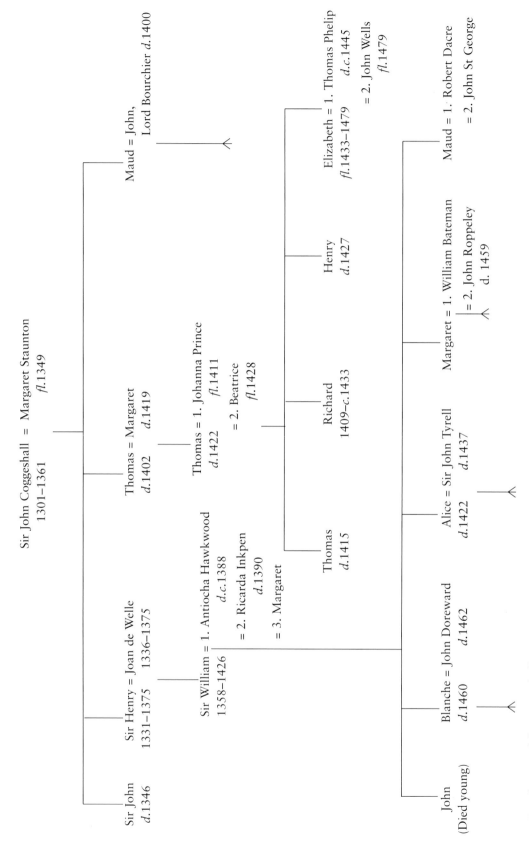

THE COGGESHALL FAMILY OF ESSEX

Family tree of the Coggeshalls.

Great Codham Hall, Wethersfield, Essex, home of Sir William Coggeshall (d.1426) and his wife Lady Antiocha (Hawkwood).   ERO: I/Mp 397/1/2

Arundel. It is not known what influence Sir William exercised on behalf of his father-in-law and whether this diminished on the death of his wife Antiocha *c.*1388 (Sir William subsequently married Ricarda Inkpen who died in 1390 and later still, a certain Margaret).[98] Little is known about Antiocha, except that she bore Sir William five children; a son John (who died young and childless) and four daughters, all of whom eventually married into prominent local gentry families. In the poll tax records of 1381 Lady Coggeshall is listed under Gosfield as 'Antiocha wife of William de Coggeshall' and taxed at three shillings and four pence, possibly indicating that she was then staying with her uncle John Hawkwood the elder and his wife Margaret (whose principal manor was in Gosfield) whilst her husband was away in London or elsewhere.[99] Her servant was taxed at twelve pence as 'Margaret, servant of Lady de Coggeshall'.

Sir John Hawkwood also had a powerful friend in Sir William Coggeshall's uncle Thomas Coggeshall (*c.*1335-1402), who may once have been a *condottiere*, but who was certainly a trusted friend at the end of Hawkwood's life.[100] Thomas Coggeshall had served in Humphrey de Bohun's retinue in France *c.*1372 and, like his nephew Sir William, was a member of Countess Joan's circle. Sir William Coggeshall had other useful Essex connections including his brother-in-law John, Lord Bourchier. Thomas Coggeshall had a modest income in comparison with his nephew but had held the office of escheator and served as a knight of the shire for Essex. Through the Coggeshall family Hawkwood would have been associated with, though not necessarily acquainted with, their neighbour John Doreward, the Essex lawyer and Speaker of the Commons whose son John Doreward was to marry Hawkwood's granddaughter Blanche Coggeshall. Doreward the elder was an important member of the Earl of Oxford's affinity and a powerful political figure in his own right.[101]

When, as an old man, Sir John Hawkwood began to plan his return to England so that he could die in his homeland, he wrote in English to his friend Thomas Coggeshall to ask his help.[102] Dated 20 February 1393, a year before his death, Hawkwood's letter addresses Thomas Coggeshall as 'Dere trusty & welbiloved frend ... the holy gost have you in his kepyng'. This certainly has an air of sincerity about it which is lacking in the formulaic greetings encountered in other letters of the period. In the same letter he refers to 'Hopky' (Robert) Rikyngdon, Jankyn (John) Serjaunt, Robert Lyndeseye and 'alle myn other frendes'. Thomas Coggeshall and John Sampson (Hawkwood's 'welbiloved squyer') signed an indenture at Coggeshall's manor of New Hall, Boreham on 20 April 1393, which set out Hawkwood's wishes for the disposal of his property in England in the event of his death, which must then have been considered to be imminent.[103]

Hawkwood had another personal squire whose name was Robert de Saxlingham and in Italy a trumpeter named Zuzzo. In 1385 there was a soldier serving with him at Cavezzi near Modena who was probably another Essex man, perhaps from his own village, one 'John Edingam, Englishman'.[104]

CHAPTER SEVEN

Hawkwood's DEATH

Just five days before he died, the *Signoria* of Florence agreed to commute for cash the pension they had been paying Sir John Hawkwood 'Considering that Hawkwood, weary by reason of his great age, and as he asserts, weighed down by infirmity, wishes to return to his old country'.[105] Hawkwood had in fact been considering his impending demise for some time because, in the trust deed executed on 20 April 1393 between his kinsman Thomas Coggeshall of Little Baddow and his squire John Sampson, his intentions 'yif he deye bifore his comyng hom' were made clear.[106]

The trust deed dealt firstly with his London property, including the Leadenhall Market, which was to be sold and the proceeds used to endow chantry priests in the convent at Castle Hedingham and in Sible Hedingham parish church. In the event, Hawkwood's directions did not take effect until long after his death in 1394. He had trustees looking after his interests in England, including: the Essex man John Sergeant; two Londoners, John Cavendish, a draper, and Robert Lyndesey, a tailor; and as his principal trustee, Robert Rikedon, the Witham lawyer who shared a successful practice in London and Essex with Clement Spice of Black Notley.[107] There is no record of how Hawkwood came to choose these trustees, or whether he knew them all personally. Kenneth Fowler has identified the movement of cash in Hawkwood's name between Italy and England, which may have enabled Hawkwood to buy his English estates (which were never sold to pay his debts in Italy).[108]

Hawkwood's proprietary interest in the Leadenhall in the City of London is comparatively well documented.[109] During the late fourteenth century the Leadenhall estate comprised a cluster of houses, shops and warehouses surrounding a provisions market, and also included the advowsons of five City churches; from *c*.1325 the Leadenhall was

Leadenhall Market, London. Sir John Hawkwood's principal property in England.
Photograph Christopher Starr

described as a manor. The reversion of the Leadenhall estate had been acquired from a group of trustees apparently acting for Lady Alesia de Neville (whose husband John de Neville of Wethersfield (*d*.1359) was a neighbour of the Coggeshalls) who retained a life interest in the property until her death in 1394. The original group of Lady Neville's trustees comprised: John Ward, citizen of London; Richard Lyons; and John, Parson of Drinkstone. Ward and John the Parson later quitclaimed their interest (including the advowsons) to Lady Alice. In 1380 Lady Alice enfeoffed Thomas Coggeshall, Robert Rikedon, John Sergeant, John Cavendish and Robert Lyndesey (all associates of Sir John Hawkwood) with the reversion of the property, presumably to the use of Sir John Hawkwood.

Sir John Hawkwood as soldier and statesman.
Uccello, Paolo (1397-1475): Monument to Sir John Hawkwood. Florence, Cathedral.
© 2002. Photo Scala, Florence

The previously mentioned indenture sealed at Boreham in 1393 also provided that if Lady Donnina Hawkwood should outlive her husband, remain unmarried thereafter, and come to England, she was to then enjoy a life interest in Sir John's manor of Listons (now Liston Hall) in Gosfield and Hostages Farm in Sible Hedingham. On her death this property was to pass to the Hawkwoods' son John junior, and in the meantime the rest of Sir John's property in England was to be held in trust for John junior until he came of age. The indenture also stipulated that in the event of John junior failing to marry and produce a *male* heir, all the English property was to be sold and the proceeds used to endow a chantry. Prayers would be said there in perpetuity for the soul of Sir John Hawkwood, and the souls of his friends – especially those 'that weren slayn for his love'. This moving phrase appears to refer to those who were killed in battle whilst under his command. Significantly, the indenture refers neither to Hawkwood's burial nor the provision of a tomb. It is not clear when or how Hawkwood acquired his Essex estates, although he appears to have purchased some of them out of his Italian earnings. He may have inherited part of this property from his elder brother who apparently predeceased him.

In Florence, the *Signoria* passed a resolution on 22 August 1393 to provide a tomb for Hawkwood in the Duomo at the city's expense. In the light of subsequent events it is interesting that they intended to

> cause to be constructed and made in the said church, and in a conspicuous place, high and honourable ... a worthy and handsome tomb for the ashes of the great and brave knight Sir John Hawkwood, English captain-general of war ... [The] said sepulchre ... in which the body of the said Sir John and no other body may be placed, shall be adorned with such stone and marble figures and armorial ensigns as shall seem convenient. [110]

For various reasons, principally perhaps of economy, this monument was never constructed. Instead, in 1436, the artist Paolo Uccello was commissioned to paint a fresco in the Duomo, Florence, which showed Hawkwood on horseback and in a martial pose. Many years later the enormous fresco was lifted off the wall and framed. Today this icon of the Renaissance hangs in the north aisle of the Duomo.[111]

After a short illness, Hawkwood died at his house in Florence during the night of 16/17 March 1394, apparently of a stroke. The citizens of Florence were sufficiently appreciative of their captain-general to give him a magnificent funeral in the Duomo. He lay in state in the Baptistery for several days, with his sword on his chest and his baton by his side, surrounded by heraldic trappings, grieving relatives, friends and citizens. There is no doubt that Hawkwood was interred in the north wall of the cathedral choir, as a document dated 16 May 1394 records the purchase of bread and wine for the mason and his assistant who resealed the tomb after it had been opened.[112] It is not clear, however, why the tomb had been opened after Hawkwood's burial. Nothing now remains of this tomb, but there are several which date from Hawkwood's time in the excavated walls of the earlier cathedral beneath the present Duomo.

When news of Hawkwood's death reached Richard II he wrote to the *Signoria* requesting the return of the Englishman's body.[113] It is worth remembering that the King and Sir John were distant kinsmen by reason of the short-lived marriage between Richard's uncle, Lionel, and Violante Visconti. The King's request regarding Hawkwood's remains should be seen in the context of what Nigel Saul has identified as Richard II's penchant for collecting the bones of famous Englishmen and having them interred in Westminster Abbey.[114] The *Signoria* acceded to the King's request and permission for Hawkwood's 'ashes' and 'bones' to be returned to England was granted on 3 June 1395.[115] There is, however, no evidence that Richard II's request was actually complied with, for the opening of Hawkwood's tomb in May 1394 appears to be unconnected with Richard II's desire to have the remains brought to England. It is possible that the bones were re-interred in Westminster Abbey or, if the King had made the request on behalf of Hawkwood's widow, the remains could have gone to Sible Hedingham for burial in the parish church. It is probably not too cynical to suggest that the *Signoria* were relieved to be spared the expense of a 'stone and marble' monument to Hawkwood,

Quintodecimo die Junii Anno regni Regis Henrici quarti post conquestum undecimo venit hic ...
... Com Essex ... ptulit maior et Aldermannis quasdam literas Thome Coggesale & Johem Hank...
... verba consequencia continentes

Dere ... grete you wel and do you to wytyn þat at the makyng of þis lre I was in god poynt ... god wol ...
I sende Johan Sampson bryngere of þis lre to you enformed of certeyn thynges whiche he schal tellyn you be
mouthe ... Wherfore I preye you þat ye lenyn hym as my pson wrytyn at Florence þe viij day of Januarij
et ... John Hanchade chivaler

Dere trusty & welbeloved frend ... I grete you wel desiryng to heren god tidynges of youre welfare &
prayng you þat ye be helpyng & consaillyng to my welbeloved squyer Jankyn Sampson touchyng þat þe he
hath to pursuen for me atte þis tyme & namelich for my sauf conduyte & touchyng my will & my pcer ...
I praye you þat ye wole youre for & gevence to the forseid Jankyn Sampson of al thilk he wole seyen you
by mouthe ... And I pray you þat ye wole speke to ... & to Jankyn Doraunt Robt hudelere &
alle other frendes þat yen don as ye forseid Jankyn Sampson seith to you touchyng my will ... Trusty
frend þe holy gost haue you in his kepyng ... at Florence þe xx day of Januer þe yer of oure
lord M CCCC xxxxij

Item quintodecimo die Junii pdco Robtus Rikedon ptulit hic eisdem maiori & Aldermannis quandam
copiam cuiusdam indenture factu inter Thomam Coggesale & Johem Sampson ... pðic John Hank...
verba consequencia continentes

This endenture mad bitwene my maister Thomas Coggesale on that on half & me John Sampson on
that othe half witnesseth that my maister Sir John Hanchade knyght bad me the forseid John
Sampson ... my gevence to you Thomas Coggesale in this wise: my maister one John
Hanchade gretyth you wel & saieth you to seyen that he puppseth hym for to comen in to
Englond ... & I am comen to pursuen ... sanfconduyte on for my maister & another my self to
men ... hors & harneys ... I wole ... to Caleys they killed that alle these lordes been
there ... & also my maister biddeth you to seyen that yif he deye before his comyng hom that
ye wolde buchbe his will what he wolde have don with the londes & tenementz that been
purchased to his bihufue in Englond for he hath ordeyned for his sogheryn in graue atte ...
he wolde that the toune halle with the apurtenaunces of the chirche be sold & ij prestes ...
in the nonnery of Hechyngham to singen there in my maistres chapel & j prest in the parissh
chirche of Hechyngham stille ... & also yif my lady Hanchade ouer lyue my maister Sir John
Hanchade & kepe hir sole & come in to Englond he preyeth you & alle the other feffees ye wolde
enfeffe hire in lisones & estates in Hechyngham to terme of hire lyf ... the revercion to John
Hanchade the eyre of hire in the tayle and the remenaunt to be kept in handes of the feffees til John
my maistres sone be of ful age And at his ful age enfeffin hym they in that is to seyen to comen to hym and
to his heires of his body goten & for defaute of issue of his body he wole that the forseid londes ben sold
& do for his sowle & for his frendes as yow thenketh best And namelich for the soules of hem that
were slayn for his loue And in the menetyme that my maistres sone is withinne age that the prestes
of the londes also be don for my maistres soule & yif my maister come hom as I hope he shal then
he wole ordeyne for hym self as hym liketh best This is wryten by me forseid John Sampson
atte the ...halle in boram in Essex the xx day of April the yer of oure lord the kyng
Richard XIo

Undecimo die Augusti Anno regni Regis Henrici quarti post conqu Undecimo venerunt hic ...
... Johem Drey & Johes Affele panmay ... London ...

and at the same time pleased to have this opportunity to improve Anglo-Florentine relations.

In 1398, Lady Hawkwood came to London to complain to Richard II about the conduct of her late husband's English trustees and the King ordered the Lord Mayor, Richard Whittington, to hear her complaint.[116] She claimed that the trustees were failing in their duty to carry out instructions and render proper accounts, and also that they had removed a box of Sir John's muniments from safe keeping in St Paul's Cathedral. From Lady Hawkwood's point of view the outcome of the hearing was inconclusive, and the trustees continued to prevaricate for many years. According to Hawkwood's wishes, the Leadenhall should have been sold as soon as possible after his death, but it was not sold until 1409 when a consortium, headed by none other than Richard Whittington, paid £566 13s. 4d. for it. Whittington later granted the Leadenhall estate to future lord mayors and the commonalty of London in perpetuity.[117] An arrangement that continues to the present day.

During her visit to England it is possible that Lady Hawkwood stayed for part of the time at the family home of Sir William Coggeshall at Great Codham Hall, Wethersfield, a few miles from Sible Hedingham. However, her step-daughter Antiocha was dead by this date and Sir William had twice since remarried. It is also possible that Lady Hawkwood brought her late husband's remains to their last resting-place in Essex when she came to England to seek justice. Lady Hawkwood is last heard of in England in 1398 and it is not known whether she returned to Italy.[118] In this context it should be remembered that her life interest in her husband's property was contingent upon her living in England and remaining unmarried.

In 1412 Robert Rikedon carried out his final duties as trustee for the Hawkwoods and thereby fulfilled the terms of the 1393 indenture. Together with his son, Robert junior, and a certain John Coo, Rikedon obtained a royal licence (dated 12 October 1412) on payment of a fee of twenty pounds, to found a chantry with one chaplain in Sible Hedingham parish church and another chantry with one priest in the nuns' priory of Castle Hedingham.[119] Morant says that the chantry house at Castle Hedingham 'was standing at the end of the town, by the right hand side of the road leading to Sudbury till 1676, when it was pulled down, and set up again for a farm-house upon some lands belonging to the late dissolved Nunnery'.[120] The licence obtained by the Rikedons required that the priests were to be employed in celebrating divine service in both locations for the souls of Sir John Hawkwood, John Oliver esquire and Thomas Newenton esquire.

The identities of Oliver and Newenton are not precisely known, but it has been suggested that they were Hawkwood's military companions. A deed of 1373, now in the Essex Record Office, shows John Oliver of Stanway as trustee of several manors including Sandon (which belonged to Thomas Coggeshall) for Thomas de Newton and his wife Elizabeth.[121] It is probable that the foundation deed of the chantry chapels, of which no record survives, included prayers for a wider circle of family, friends and associates. In order to provide a sufficient endowment, four messuages, four tofts and almost five hundred acres of land were amortised by Hawkwood's trustees. This appears to have comprised the remainder of the Hawkwood family's estates in England. Clearly, in selling the Hawkwood patrimony in compliance with the 1393 indenture, the trustees signified that Sir John's male heirs were extinct and that John junior had died before October 1412.[122]

Opposite Copies of correspondence from Sir John Hawkwood and John Sampson enrolled in the records of the City of London. Plea and Memoranda Roll A41, membrane 8, paras 1-5.

By kind permission of Guildhall Library, City of London Corporation

Measured drawing of Sir John Hawkwood's tomb at Sible Hedingham from Frederic Chancellor's Ancient Sepulchral Monuments of Essex *(1890).*

CHAPTER EIGHT

Hawkwood's TOMB

From the surviving architectural evidence in Sible Hedingham church, it is likely that Sir John Hawkwood's trustees appropriated an existing aisle and adapted it for use as a chantry. It was one of several hundred medieval chantries founded in the Diocese of London. The principal feature of the new chantry was, of course, the tomb of the founder, which was placed centrally in the south wall of the aisle. At the east end, below a window, was an altar where masses were sung every day by the chantry priest for the repose of Hawkwood's soul. At the west end of the aisle may have been the priest's accommodation, his duties and office being separate from those of the parish priest. Beside the altar, also in the south wall, was a piscina which remains in its original position. There was probably a wooden screen separating the chantry from the nave. Little else is known of the original chantry fittings, but what is almost certainly Hawkwood's tomb remains largely intact. The Hawkwood monument is one of twenty-four recessed tombs in Essex which date from the fourteenth and fifteenth centuries.[123]

Seen in context, a chantry was both a memorial to the dead and a statement of the family's social position; daily masses for the founder's soul kept not only him, but also his family in mind in the locality. The close proximity of Hawkwood's chantry to the badges and escutcheons of the de Vere and Bourchier families in window glass, floor tiles and roof bosses emphasised the Hawkwoods' connection with, and implied approval by, the higher nobility of Essex.

The arms of the Bateman, Coggeshall and Hawkwood families in stained glass surviving from a fifteenth-century memorial in St Mary the Virgin's Church, Little Sampford, Essex.

A fourteenth-century slip tile, depicting a hawk, loose in St Peter's Church, Sible Hedingham, thought to have come from the Hawkwood chantry.

Photographs Clare Banks

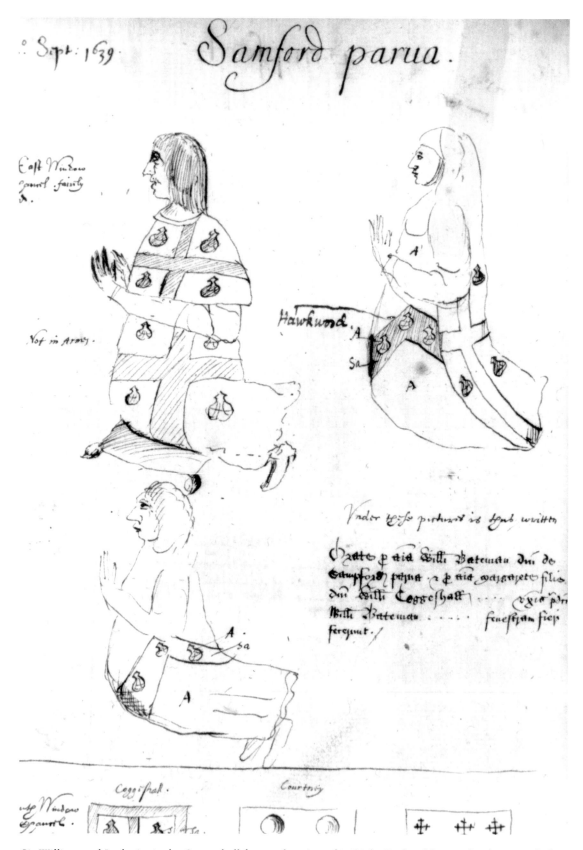

Sir William and Lady Antiocha Coggeshall from a drawing of 1639 by Richard Symonds of a stained glass window formerly in St Mary the Virgin's Church, Little Sampford, Essex. College of Arms, Symonds MS Essex 2.

By kind permission of the College of Arms

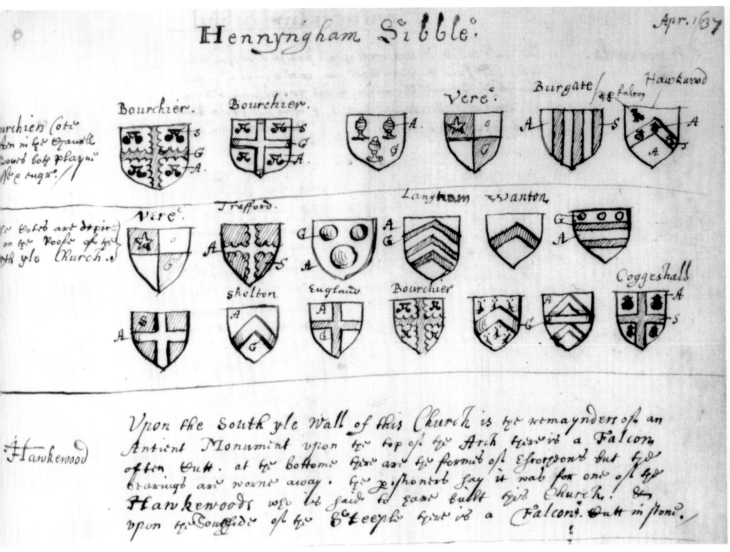

Description by Richard Symonds, in 1637, of Sir John Hawkwood's tomb and heraldic glass formerly in St Peter's Church, Sible Hedingham, Essex. College of Arms Symonds MS Essex 2.

By kind permission of the College of Arms

The Hawkwood family, which had so recently risen to the ranks of the gentry, utilised these symbols to signify its new position in the social hierarchy. Several loose slipware tiles have been found in the vestry of the church; one in particular is decorated with a hawk and it appears to date from the end of the fourteenth century; it may once have been set in the chantry floor. The tile is similar to one to be found in the church at Bradwell-juxta-Coggeshall, a few miles from Sible Hedingham.[124]

The earliest surviving description of the Hawkwood tomb is that given by John Stow in *Annales of England* (1605), in which, after mentioning Hawkwood's 'tomb' in Florence 'with the Image of a man on horseback, as great as a

mightie Pillar', he went on to describe more accurately 'a Monument, or Tombe arched over, and ingraven to the likenesse of Haukes flying in a woode, in the Parish Church of Hingham Sible'.[125] John Weever, in his *Funerall Monuments* (1631), gives an almost identical description to Stow, but asserts that the tomb at Sible Hedingham had vanished long before his own time.[126] The first known eyewitness description of the monument was made by the soldier and antiquary Richard Symonds of Great Yeldham. Symonds recorded in his notebook on 13 April 1637: 'Upon the south yle Wall of this Church is the remaynders of an Ancient Monument upon the top of the Arch there is a Falcon ... The p[ar]ishoners say it was

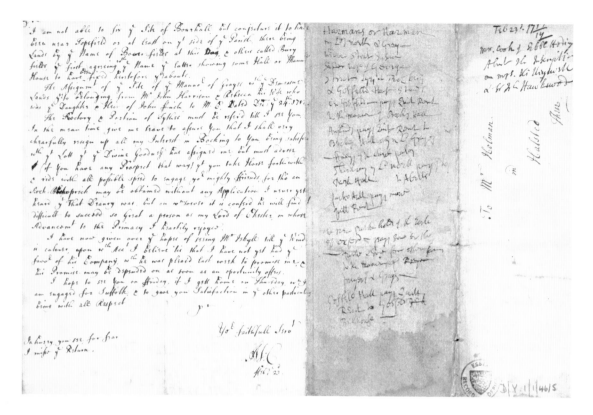

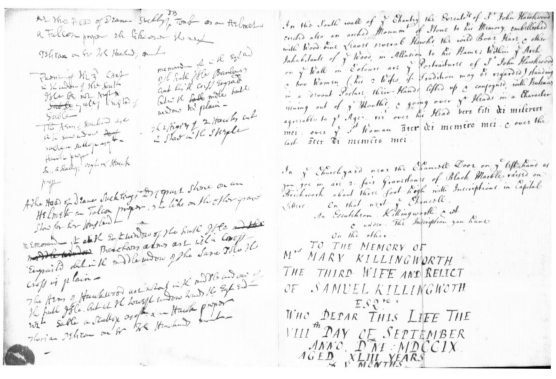

A letter dated 23 February 1714 from Moses Cooke, Rector of Sible Hedingham to the antiquary William Holman of Halstead, in which he describes the Hawkwood tomb, including the wall painting. Holman has endorsed both sides of the letter with further information about the church. ERO: D/Y 1/1/46/7

for one of the Hawkewoods who it is said … built this Church'.[127] He also made drawings of the then surviving heraldic stained glass relating to Hawkwood and his family connections in the windows of the aisle.

Almost a century later, a much more detailed account of the monument was written (but not published) by William Holman of Halstead, a dissenting minister and antiquary who died in 1730.[128] Holman apparently acquired most of his information about the monument from Moses Cooke, Rector of Sible Hedingham (1690-1733), who wrote to him on 23 April 1713 that: 'I am advised to clean the Monum[en]t of S[i]r John Hawkwood with warm water w[hi]ch had been done before this if the severity of the weather w[oul]d have permitted, & th[e]n you shall command w[ha]t is legible th[e]reon.'[129] By 23 February 1714, the Rector had probably washed the dirt-encrusted paintings on the monument for he wrote to Holman that day with the following description of them:

> In the South wall of the Chantry the Executors of S[i]r John Hawkwood erected also an arched Monum[en]t of Stone to his Memory, embellished with Wood-bine Leaves, several Hawks, the Wild Boar, Hare, & other inhabitants of the Wood, in Allusion to his Name: Within the Arch on the Wall in Colours are the Portraitures of S[i]r John Hawkwood & two Women (his 2 Wifes, if Tradition may be regarded) standing in a devout Posture, their Hands lifted up & conjoyned, with Sentences issuing out of th[ei]r Mouths & going over th[ei]r Heads in a Character agreeable to th[a]t Age viz over his Head *vere fili dei miserere mei* over the 1st Woman *ater dei meme[n]to mei* & over the last *ater xi meme[n]to mei*.[130]

This record of a wall painting associated with Hawkwood is particularly valuable, as the Rector's description is likely to be authentic, if not necessarily accurate. Holman thought it so, and incorporated it almost verbatim in his folder of notes on Sible Hedingham parish church. He added, perhaps from his own observation, that

'from the effigies on this monument it should seem that he had two wives'.[131] Was he describing the wall painting, sculptures, or even monumental brasses? Today, there is no sign of the paintings, and if anything still remains it is covered by many layers of limewash and distemper. There is nothing in Essex that resembles the medieval paintings described by Moses Cooke, but there are contemporary examples elsewhere.

Philip Morant apparently took Holman's notes on the monument at face value and repeated them in his *History and Antiquities of the County of Essex* (1768). This working method was criticised by the antiquary Richard Gough, for in his opinion Morant was merely an armchair antiquary. Gough had written, with reference to Morant, that 'recluse and sedentary antiquarians find it much easier to arrange materials put into their hands than to ramble about the country and examine every remain of antiquity'.[132] Morant's extensive use of Holman's notes suggests that he may never have visited Sible Hedingham, except that he wrote: 'The old Church that stood there before, was much less, as hath appeared by the foundations that have been discovered', perhaps because he had seen them for himself.[133]

In *Memoirs of Sir John Hawkwood* (1782) Richard Gough justly criticises Thomas Fuller who in his *History of the Worthies of England* (1662) simply copied Weever's assertion that the Hawkwood monument had vanished.[134] Gough admonished him for not taking 'any pains to visit or procure true information about this monument, which still remains in good preservation near the upper end of the south isle'. Clearly he was exasperated by fellow antiquaries who did not care to get their boots dirty in the pursuit of evidence. He then observed that on the tomb slab

> which is of grey marble, are some imperfect traces of figures inlaid in brass; but not enough to support Mr Morant's assertion, that 'from the effigies on this monument it should seem [that] he had two wives'. Within the arch were some lines painted on the wall by way of epitaph, but they have been whited over, and are not preserved in any author.[135]

This print is the earliest known illustration of Sir John Hawkwood's tomb at Sible Hedingham, from a drawing made in 1775 and published in 'Memoirs of Sir John Hawkwood', Biographica Topographica Britannia (1782).

Gough also described the glass at Sible Hedingham: 'In a south window of the chantry chapel, at the east end of this isle [sic], are painted hawks, hawks bells, and escallops, which last are part of the Hawkwood arms'. Like Morant, Gough mentions the hawks carved in stone on the church tower. Included in *Memoirs* is an engraving showing the monument 'from a drawing taken on the spot 1775 by the late ingenious Mr Tyson'; this is the earliest known representation of the monument.

During the nineteenth century a number of antiquaries visited Sible Hedingham church and noted the appearance of the Hawkwood monument.[136] In his *Ancient Sepulchral Monuments of Essex* (1890) the architect Frederic Chancellor published measured drawings of the tomb, together with the following vivid description:

> The monument is of stone of the late Decorated period, the carving is bold and spirited. In the four large spandrils in tracery are carved a Boar in foliage, (in allusion to his friend De Vere), a hawk, belled, in foliage (a punning allusion to his name), a pelican feeding her young, and another bird, probably intended for a hawk in foliage; there is something attached to one leg, but it is not so distinctly a hawk bell as in the other spandril. In the small spandrils are a wild animal with long head and long thick tail (perhaps a fox in allusion to his craftiness), a coney and a figure blowing a horn, a wild naked man and foliage, and in one is a small implement like a cruet, perhaps intended to represent something in connection with hawks. The foliage is very decorated in character, and the crockets and finials are very spirited and good.[137]

Chancellor also refers to the absence of an inscription or brasses and says: 'The whole is now covered with a thick coat of light blue distemper'.

Toward the end of the nineteenth century the monument was enclosed with panelling so as to make a large box pew for one of the more

Monument to Sir John Thornbury (d.1396), All Saints' Church, Little Munden, Hertfordshire. Hawkwood's enemy and former second-in-command. Photograph Christopher Starr

substantial families in Sible Hedingham. The wall at the back of the tomb was partially covered by a wainscot panel and several remaining dowel holes show where it was attached. It is not known when this pew was dismantled and removed, but it can be seen in a photograph taken *c*.1920.[138]

Today the tomb remains in good condition. There are still traces of the 'blue distemper' noticed by Chancellor, as well as medieval polychromy. The surface of the tomb slab bears a number of metal rivets, indents and innumerable graffiti, but it is not clear from this evidence whether there were monumental brasses. On the back wall of the tomb where small areas of modern limewash have been chipped off, layers of different coloured pigment are visible, some of which may date from Hawkwood's time.

Despite its apparent anonymity, the monument's punning carvings clearly relate to a member of the Hawkwood family. Whether it commemorates Sir John Hawkwood (either as a cenotaph or a tomb) may never be known, but the weight of architectural, antiquarian and anecdotal evidence suggests that it does. It is possible that the tomb also commemorates other members of the Hawkwood family, perhaps Sir John Hawkwood's son John junior who may have been buried at Sible Hedingham c.1412. Such monuments are particularly hard to date as popular designs often continued in use for many years.[139] Its appearance is, however, consistent with the period 1380-1420 and as such it is unlikely to commemorate Sir John's father Gibert de Hawkwood. At Little Munden, Hertfordshire, the tomb of Hawkwood's rival *condottiere* Sir John Thornbury, who died in 1396, not only provides a comparison with the monument at Sible Hedingham, but also allows a tantalizing glimpse of how Hawkwood might have appeared in contemporary armour.[140]

If the essentially medieval monument at Sible Hedingham is indeed Sir John Hawkwood's, there is absolutely nothing about it that reminds us of his career as a *condottiere* in Italy, indeed the contrast with Uccello's painting is particularly marked. So too is the contrast between the magnificence of the Duomo in Florence where he was buried, and the simple parish church in Essex where his remains may eventually have come to rest. Nevertheless the modest chantry that Hawkwood's trustees provided for him at Sible Hedingham reflects, in English terms at least, his high rank and status as a knight. It is also a memorial to his dynasty which, having risen from unfree to gentry status in two or three generations, then failed in the male line with equal rapidity. ▨

Above *Detail from Sir John Hawkwood's tomb at Sible Hedingham. A belled hawk surrounded by foliage, an allusion to the Hawkwood family.*

Opposite *The south aisle, formerly the Hawkwood Chantry Chapel, Sible Hedingham, with Sir John Hawkwood's tomb in the south wall.*   Photographs Clare Banks

The chancel, chancel arch and nave, St Peter's Church, Sible Hedingham.   Photograph Clare Banks

CHAPTER NINE

Hawkwood's POSTERITY

Nothing is known about Hawkwood's two sons by his presumed first wife except that they were held hostage in the city of Bologna in 1375 and that they were released unharmed to their father. As to their sisters, the eldest was Antiocha, who married Sir William Coggeshall of Great Codham Hall, Wethersfield and by whom she had a son, John, and four daughters. Hawkwood's second daughter was Fiorentina, who married Lancellotto del Mayno; the third daughter was Beatrice who married John Shelley, the reputed ancestor of the poet Percy Bysshe Shelley. Hawkwood's wife Donnina Visconti had four children: John junior; Giannetta who married Brezaglia, son of Count Ludivico di Porciglia in 1392; Caterina who married Konrad von Prassberg in 1393; and Anna who married Ambrogiulo di Piero della Torre.[141]

All the daughters of Antiocha Hawkwood married prominent members of the gentry. Blanche (d.1460) married John Doreward of Bocking; Alice (d.1422) married Sir John Tyrell of East Horndon; Margaret married first William Bateman of Little Sampford, then John Roppeley; and Maud who married first Robert Dacre, then John St George. Alice Tyrell, like her Hawkwood great-grandmother, named two of her sons John (and two William). Twenty or more families in the peerage are descended from Antiocha's four daughters; in 1890 these descendants included a duke, three marquises, sixteen earls and seven barons.[142]

In addition to the two groups of children already described, Sir John Hawkwood had a bastard son, John, by a woman whose name is not known. He was born c.1350-1355, for in June 1373 Gregory IX ordered the Bishop of London to enquire into the fitness of John, scholar and natural son of John Hawkwood knight, and to ordain him, despite his illegitimacy, 'provided he be not an imitator of his father's incontinency'.[143] In 1373 Hawkwood was in the Pope's service so he no doubt looked for a favourable outcome to this application for a papal licence.

We do not know when Sir John and Lady Hawkwood's son John was born. John junior was still a minor at the time of Hawkwood's death, so the Hawkwood patrimony was partly held in dower by his widow (who was alive in 1398, but whose date of death is not known) and partly by a group of trustees. The next we hear of John junior is that in 1406, having been born in Italy, he was granted denization in England for a fee of forty shillings by Henry IV.[144] It is not known where Lady Hawkwood and her son John junior spent the years after Sir John's death, but it is probable that they lived either in Florence (where funds would have been in short supply), or in Essex where they had rental income. John junior obtained seisin of his Essex estate in 1409 and this indicates that he had either attained the age of twenty-one (and was therefore born c.1388) or his mother died during that year and her property reverted to John junior.[145] In addition to being his father's heir, it is possible that John junior was also heir to his uncle, John Hawkwood the elder of Gosfield, who seems to have outlived his own son John.[146]

John Hawkwood the elder's principal property appears to have been Gosfield Hall (possibly inherited from his father). The house has since been rebuilt several times and is located across the fields from the parish church. The Hawkwoods of Gosfield also held the manors of Park Hall in Gosfield, Blois in Sible Hedingham, Berwicks in Toppesfield and Padbury in Buckinghamshire, although some of this property was held in trust for Sir John. As has been said, Sir John also held the Leadenhall in London, Hostages in Sible Hedingham and a portion of Liston Hall in Gosfield.[147]

SIR JOHN HAWKWOOD AND HIS CHILDREN

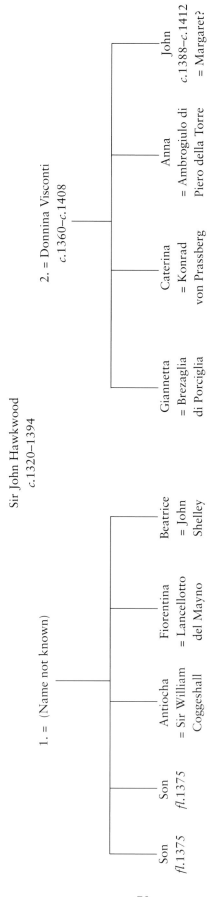

Sir John Hawkwood
*c.*1320–1394

1. = (Name not known)

2. = Donnina Visconti
*c.*1360–*c.*1408

Son
*fl.*1375

Son
*fl.*1375

Antiocha
= Sir William
Coggeshall

Fiorentina
= Lancellotto
del Mayno

Beatrice
= John
Shelley

Giannetta
= Brezaglia
di Porciglia

Caterina
= Konrad
von Prassberg

Anna
= Ambrogiulo di
Piero della Torre

John
*c.*1388–*c.*1412
= Margaret?

Sir John Hawkwood's family.

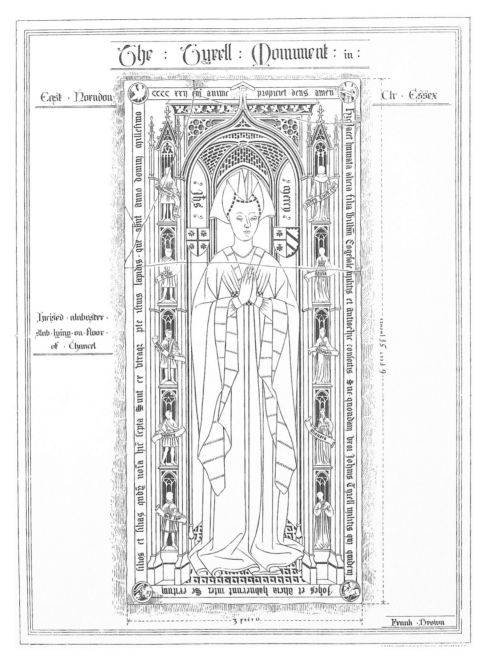

Lady Alice Tyrell (d.1422) Hawkwood's granddaughter, commemorated by an incised slab at All Saints' Church, East Horndon, Essex, from Frederic Chancellor's Ancient Sepulchral Monuments of Essex *(1890).*

It seems that John the elder died before his brother Sir John and that his own son John had predeceased him some time after 1367. In this event John the elder's land would have passed first to his wife Margaret (assuming she had not already died) and then to any surviving children.

On 22 July 1409, after the sale of the Leadenhall to Richard Whittington and others, Robert Rikedon, Sir John's trustee and administrator of his estate, quitclaimed the property he had held on his behalf to John junior. This included the manors of Blois in Sible Hedingham (previously held by John the elder as feoffee for Sir John), Liston Hall in Gosfield (apparently held previously by Sir John), Hodings in Gosfield and Hawkwoods in Gosfield (present day Hawkwoods Farm), together with properties in Gosfield, Sible Hedingham, Halstead, Castle Hedingham, Great Maplestead, Bocking, Stisted and Wethersfield. Also Hostages, Sible

Gosfield Hall, home of the Hawkwood family and their successors, the Rolfs.   ERO: 1/Mp 155/1/4

Hedingham (the farm formerly held by Sir John) and all 'lands, rents and services' in Sible Hedingham called 'Potterestrete' (doubtless the Hawkwood's ancestral home, and now known as Hawkwood Manor).[148]

The day before, on 21 July, John Hawkwood junior and Rikedon quitclaimed the manor of Padbury (otherwise Millbury) in Buckinghamshire to John Barton the younger, having previously leased the property to Barton in September 1408, after which it had been leased back to Rikedon.[149] On 26 September 1409, a further transaction took place for the benefit of John junior when Robert Rikedon and John Sampson transferred the Toppesfield manors of Scotneys and Berwicks, with which John the elder had been enfeoffed in 1380, to a group of trustees who included Sir William Coggeshall, John Doreward and Clement Spice.[150] His deceased half-sister's husband Sir William Coggeshall and others were to hold the manor in trust for 'John Hawkwood, son of John Hawkwood knight', for him and his wife in tail if he should marry in the next five years, if he should not, then to settle on him in tail within the next two months. If he should die childless or on failure of issue, then it was to revert to Robert Rikedon senior, John and Simon Sampson, Robert Rikedon junior, Roger Spice and others as trustees.

The last known precisely dated reference to John Hawkwood esquire, otherwise John Hawkwood junior, is of 3 May 1412 and is a licence for him and others, including the Bishop of London, John de Boys, Robert de Tey, Robert Rikedon, Robert, Parson of Sible Hedingham, Richard Waltham and Thomas Rolf, to found a perpetual chantry in Halstead church for Robert, Lord Bourchier and other members of his family.[151] Lord Bourchier was John junior's distant kinsman and his tomb is still to be seen in Halstead church.

John junior is also mentioned in returns for a tax levied in 1412 when, as probably the last male of his line, he was taxed in respect of his properties in Gosfield, Sible Hedingham, Toppesfield and

Thomas Rolf (d.1440), sergeant-at-law whose monumental brass is at St Katherine's Church, Gosfield, Essex. Rolf may have married the heiress to the Hawkwood family of Gosfield and Sible Hedingham.

ERO: I/Mp 155/1/2

THE HAWKWOOD/ROLF/GREENE CONNECTION

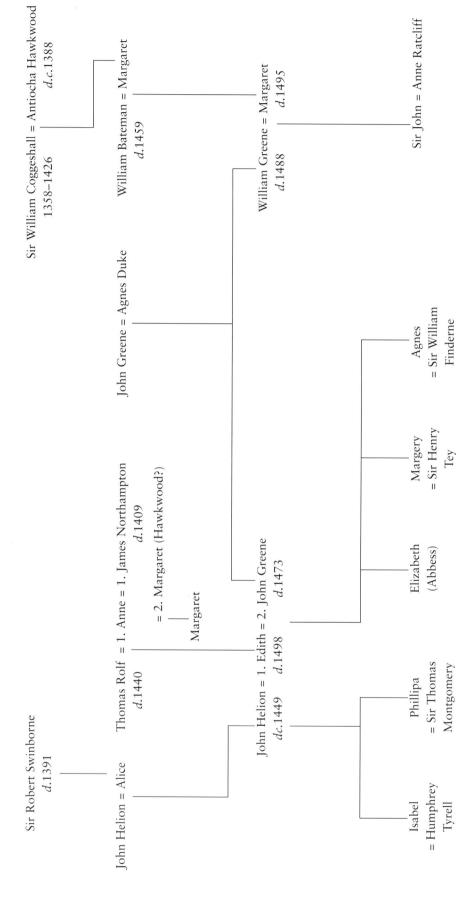

The Hawkwood, Rolf and Greene families.

Havering.[152] His landed income was estimated at that time to be fifty pounds per annum, a considerable sum and one that qualified him for knighthood; it also made him liable for county office. There is, however, no record that he was knighted or that he ever held office in Essex or elsewhere. In the absence of evidence to the contrary, it is probable that he died relatively young, aged about twenty-four, and without male issue c.1412.

There is, however, circumstantial evidence that John Hawkwood junior may have left a daughter. Much of his patrimony subsequently came into the hands of Thomas Rolf, sergeant-at-law, who settled at Gosfield Hall (previously the seat of John Hawkwood the elder). The manors of Hodings and Liston Hall in Gosfield, and Hawkwood's Farm in Gosfield appear to have passed directly (with no known intermediate owner) from John junior to Thomas Rolf, who also acquired the manor of Graveshall in Sible Hedingham and other properties in the vicinity. The method by which Rolf acquired the Hawkwood patrimony is not clear, but there are several possibilities: by purchase from the Hawkwoods' heirs (Rolf was a rich man who could doubtless have raised the purchase price); by marriage to a Hawkwood widow or heiress; or by inheritance from a Hawkwood heiress – for example, Rolf's mother may have been a Hawkwood. It is not known when Rolf came into possession of the Hawkwood lands, but it is clear that it occurred between 1412, when John junior was taxed on their account, and 1428 when Rolf was taxed on the same properties.[153]

Thomas Rolf may have been born in Essex where the name was common in the fourteenth century, or perhaps in London where the Rolfs also flourished. A namesake, possibly his father, was Thomas Rolf, a skinner and citizen of London.[154] Thomas Rolf of Essex was an apprentice-at-law during the last decade of the fourteenth century and beyond, but on 11 July 1415 he was ordered (on pain of an enormous fine of one thousand pounds) to become a sergeant-at-law, the approximate equivalent of a modern Queen's Counsel, which he did after some two years' prevarication on 1 July 1417.[155] Rolf is first heard of in an Essex connection in

1404 when he acted as a feoffee for land in the north-west of the county.[156] In the same year he twice stood surety for Sir Bartholomew Bourchier, but at this date it is difficult to distinguish him from his namesake the citizen and skinner of London who could also be persuaded to stand surety from time-to-time.[157] In 1408, he had power of attorney for Sir William Marney of Layer Marney who travelled to Ireland that year.[158]

In 1414, Rolf served as a royal commissioner with the Earl of Oxford and a number of Essex gentry, including William Bourchier, Sir William Marney, Sir William Coggeshall, Richard Baynard, Robert Rikedon and the sheriff, concerning the arrest of Lollards.[159] In the same year he was a feoffee for William Bourchier and his wife Anne, indicating that, as a rising lawyer with interests in Essex, he was an important member of the Bourchier affinity.[160] The Bourchiers had, of course, long been connected with Sible Hedingham and it may have been at their table that Rolf gleaned news of available properties in Gosfield and Sible Hedingham. He was appointed a justice of the peace in 1416 and was later a prominent member of the Earl of Oxford's affinity; it was not uncommon for the gentry to move from one affinity to another, or even to belong to two affinities at the same time.[161] In 1429, he stood surety for de Vere when he was fined two thousand pounds by the King for marrying Sir John Howard's daughter Elizabeth without licence.[162] Rolf subsequently became a justice of assize and died in late June or early July 1440. He was buried at Gosfield, quite possibly in the same church as John Hawkwood senior.[163]

Rolf married at least twice. On 17 February 1410 he spent ten pounds obtaining a royal pardon for himself and his wife Anne, widow of James Northampton, a tenant-in-chief, who held land directly from the King, on account of their trespass in marrying without licence.[164] Anne's maiden name is not known, she may possibly have been a Hawkwood. On 25 April 1410, Anne was assigned dower of the land in Middlesex and elsewhere which had belonged to her former husband.[165] The inquisition post mortem for James Northampton (dated 18 May 1409, just

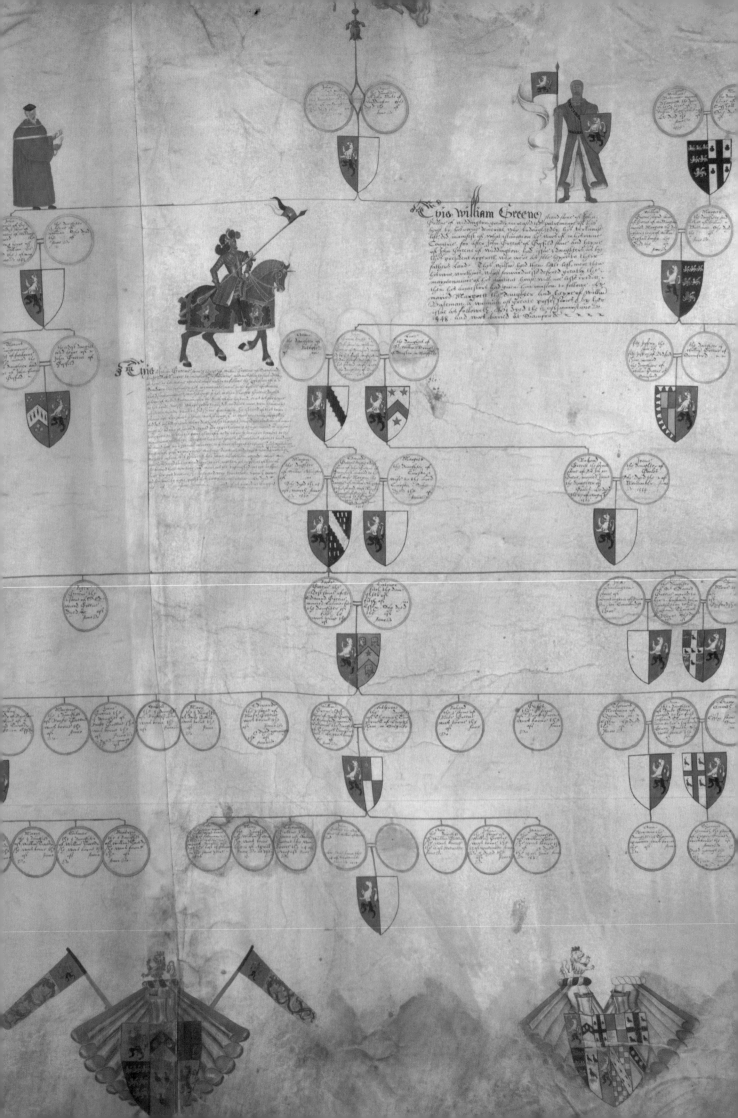

Above *A pair of label stops on the north and south sides respectively of the chancel arch, St Katherine's Church, Gosfield, Essex. They appear to indicate a union between the Rolf and Hawkwood families.*

Photographs Clare Banks

Opposite *Pedigree of 1589 showing the Greene family of Gosfield and elsewhere (see page 74).*

ERO: D/Du 1280/1

two days after his death) shows that he was the son of John Northampton and that his heir (Anne and James having no surviving children – though a dead child, Edith, is mentioned in his will), was his cousin William Comberton, then aged six, his uncle's grandson.[166]

The property that Anne received in dower was described as a messuage and a fardel in Northampton with an annual value of six shillings and eight pence, one-third of the manor of Tottenham with an annual value of eighteen pounds and other lands and tenements in Middlesex with an annual value of six pounds, thirteen shillings and four pence, together with tenements in London valued at fifteen pounds per annum; a total annual income of forty pounds per annum. James Northampton's father was John Northampton, a draper who had served as Lord Mayor of London in 1381. By his will dated 17 December 1397, John Northampton (alias Comberton) left the bulk of his property to his son

James, although he remembered other relatives too.[167] He also left a substantial sum of money to the Hospital of St Mary de Elsyngspitel within Cripplegate on the condition that they maintained a chantry for the welfare of his soul, the souls of his parents, two wives and others.

Thomas and Anne Rolf had one child and they named her Edith, possibly after the dead child of Anne's first marriage. Rolf's daughter was subsequently his sole heir and first married John Helion from the ancient Essex gentry family of that name. After the death of John Helion *c.*1449, she married John Greene, a lawyer of Widdington, who died in 1473.[168] Edith Greene died in 1498 aged, perhaps, ninety years. The Greenes and the Hawkwoods were distantly connected by marriage as John Greene's brother William (*d.*1488) married Margaret Bateman the daughter of William Bateman and his wife Margaret (Coggeshall), one of Sir John Hawkwood's granddaughters, who died in 1495.

It is not known when Anne Rolf died, but her husband Thomas had a second wife named Margaret.[169] Nothing is known about her, but it is possible that she was a member of the Hawkwood family, perhaps the daughter or widow of Sir John's son John junior (father and son are both mentioned as 'benefactors' in Rolf's will) or the daughter or granddaughter of John Hawkwood the elder of Gosfield.[170]

Evidence for a Rolf/Hawkwood marriage is circumstantial. There is, for example, the heraldry in Gosfield church. On either side of the chancel arch there is a label stop in the form of an angel holding an escutcheon. On the south side the arms are unquestionably those of Hawkwood, and on the north side the arms appear be those of Rolf (a raven). There is considerable doubt about this however, for the bird may not be a raven (it compares poorly with the raven on the shield of arms on Rolf's tomb) and may instead be a hawk. If the bird is a raven, then the heraldry most probably denotes the marriage of a Hawkwood with a Rolf, that is

Thomas Rolf and his first or second wife, but if it is a hawk (and it resembles the hawks on the tomb in Sible Hedingham church), then it denotes that a Hawkwood, presumably John Hawkwood the elder, was responsible for the rebuilding of a substantial part of the church – as seems likely. A further confusion is that the arms of the Coggeshall family are also to be found on the Rolf tomb – suggesting that one of his wives was a Coggeshall (and also therefore a kinswoman of the Hawkwoods and the Bourchiers).[171] There is no record of a Rolf/Coggeshall marriage, but Rolf's mother or either of his wives could have been a member of the Coggeshall family of London.

The last recorded Essex members of the Hawkwood family who could have been born in Sir John's lifetime are Reginald Hawkwood of Chelmsford, who was feoffee of land in Springfield in 1433, and Henry Hawkwood who, with his wife Christina, was alive in Colchester in 1458.[172] Their connection with Sir John, if any, is not known.

ABBREVIATED REFERENCES

The following abbreviations are used in the notes:

Ag.Hist.Rev.	Agricultural History Review
B.I.H.R.	Bulletin of the Institute of Historical Research
B.L.	British Library, London
C.B.A.	Council for British Archaeology
C.C.L.	Commissary Court of London
Cat.Anc. Deeds	Catalogue of Ancient Deeds
E.A.H.	Essex Archaeology and History (Transactions of the Essex Society for Archaeology and History)
E.H.R.	English History Review
Ec.H.R.	Economic History Review
E.R.O.	Essex Record Office, Chelmsford
G.L.	Guildhall Library
Med.Arch.	Medieval Archaeology
M.L.N.	Modern Language Notes
N.A.	National Archives
P.C.C.	Prerogative Court of Canterbury
P&P	Past & Present
P.R.O.	Public Record Office (now The National Archives)
R.C.H.M.	Royal Commission on Historical Monuments
T.E.A.S.	Transactions of the Essex Archaeological Society
Trans.M.B.S.	Transactions of the Monumental Brass Society
T.R.H.S.	Transactions of the Royal Historical Society
V.C.H.	Victoria County History

NOTES

Introduction

1 a) In his account of Sir John Hawkwood, Morant says: 'He was born in this village in the reign of K. Edward II. Of honest parents, his father Gilbert Hawkwood being by occupation a tanner'. P. Morant, *The History and Antiquities of the County of Essex* (2 vols, 1763-1768 repr., 1978), 2, p. 287. b) See also J. Cherry, 'Leather', in J. Blair and N. Ramsey, eds, *English Medieval Industries: Craftsmen, Techniques, Products* (1991), pp. 295-318. c) 'Heningham-Sible. This Town is made most famous by being the Birth-place of Sir John Hawkwood, the son of Gilbert Hawkwood, a Tanner here. He was bound Apprentice to a Taylor ...'. *Magna Britannia et Hibernia* I (1720), pp. 714-15.

2 The Italian proverb *Inglese italianato è un diavolo incarnato* is supposed to have originated at the time of Sir John Hawkwood and his fellow English *condottieri*.

3 Paraphrase of the account given in F.S. Saunders, *Hawkwood* (2004), p. 154.

4 T. Fuller, *Worthies of Essex* I (1840 edn.), p. 513.

5 a) For the first full-length biography of Hawkwood see J. Temple-Leader and G. Marcotti, *Sir John Hawkwood (L'Acuto): Story of a Condottiere* (Trans. Leader Scott) (1889). This is excellent for Hawkwood's career and prints many original documents, but says little about Hawkwood's Essex connections. b) A few letters written by Hawkwood are to be found in British archives eg B.L., Cott. Ch. IV.16 signed by 'John Hawkwood captain general' to the 'Defensors' of Siena *c*.1377; the seal has not survived. c) See also G. Holmes, 'Florence and the Great Schism', *Proceedings of the British Academy* 75 (1989), pp. 291-312, 'There are in fact still hundreds of unpublished letters in the archives of Florence, Siena, Lucca and elsewhere recording dealings with Hawkwood and he remains a great unsung villain, neglected by the Italians as a despicable barbarian and by the English as a pretentious adventurer.'

Hawkwood's Career

6 B.L., Harl. Ch. 51.D.6. Will of Gilbert de Hawkwood. In 1340 John Hawkwood junior was old enough to be appointed as his father's executor and was therefore born *c*.1320.

7 A sixth manor, Hawkwood's, was recognised as such in the early fifteenth century.

8 Gilbert Hawkwood's house, now known as Hawkwood Manor, in Swan Street (formerly Potter Street).

9 John de Bousser (otherwise Bourchier) was Rector of Sible Hedingham in 1328, if not before, see *Index of Placita de Banco AD 1327-1328*, Part 1 PRO Lists and Indexes 32 (1909), p. 134.

Hawkwood's Career continued

[10] The *caput* of the Bourchier family was the manor of Stansted in Halstead.

[11] a) There is a persistent tradition that Hawkwood was apprenticed to a tailor in London before beginning his military career. There is no evidence for this and the tradition may have arisen from his later association with London drapers and tailors, together with his origins in a village which was in the centre of the Essex cloth manufacturing area. It may also result from a pun on '*Acuto*', the Italian form of his name meaning inter alia 'needle'. b) In L.C. Hector and B.F. Harvey, eds, *The Westminster Chronicle 1381-1394* (1982), pp. 518-20 the chronicler confidently asserts that Hawkwood had been apprenticed to a London hosier 'dominus Johannes Haukewode qui de paupere apprenticio caligarii London'. The chronicle was written within about three years of Hawkwood's death and for January 1386 (p. 157) records the following anecdote: 'About the beginning of this month a squire who had for some time been in the company of Sir John Hawkwood in Lombardy arrived at the king's court [Richard II] with a story about a man of religion living in those parts, who predicted that within the ensuing three years the English nation, because of its evil life, would be mercilessly punished, chiefly, so he said, by famine and pestilence, but after this the country would be the happiest of all kingdoms...' c) The Worshipful Company of Merchant Taylors in London claimed Hawkwood as one of their own, arguing that he 'sprang from the lowest sphere of life, and became by the force of his own character a man of accepted position before his death'. C.M. Clode, *The Early History of the Guild of Merchant Taylors* (1888), p. 5.

[12] T. Johnes, ed., *Sir John Froissart's Chronicles* 2 (1804) p. 305.

[13] Accounts of Hawkwood's military career are to be found in the following: J. Temple-Leader and G. Marcotti, *Sir John Hawkwood (L'Acuto): Story of a Condottiere* (Trans. Leader Scott) (1889); F. Gaupp, 'The Condottiere John Hawkwood', *History* 23 (1938-9), pp. 305-21; G. Trease, *The Condottieri* (1970); B.W. Tuchman, *A Distant Mirror* (1987); K. Fowler, 'Sir John Hawkwood and the English condottieri in Trecento Italy', *Renaissance Studies*, 12 (1998), pp. 131-48; K. Fowler, *Medieval Mercenaries* 1 (2001) and *Medieval Mercenaries* 2 (Forthcoming 2008); F.S. Saunders, *Hawkwood* (2004).

[14] Hector and Harvey, *Westminster Chronicle*.

[15] Preface to R. Brown, ed., *State Papers and Manuscripts Relating to English Affairs Existing in the Archives and Collections of Venice* I 1202-1509 (1864), p. lxxvi.

[16] *Calendar of Patent Rolls* 1377-1381, p. 435.

[17] M.M. Crow and C.C. Olson, eds, *Chaucer Life Records* (1960), pp. 36-40 and 54-56 and J.M. Manly, 'Chaucer's mission to Lombardy', *Modern Language Notes* (1934), pp. 209-216; also R.A. Pratt, 'Geoffrey Chaucer, Esq., and Sir John Hawkwood', *Journal of English Literary History* 16 (1949), pp. 188-193.

[18] J.S. Roskell, L. Clark and C. Rawcliffe, eds, *The History of Parliament: The House of Commons 1386-1421* (4 vols, 1992), 4, pp. 591-3.

[19] R. Brown, ed., *State Papers and Manuscripts relating to English Affairs in Venice, 1202-1509* (1864), p. 26.

[20] *Calendar of Inquisitions Post Mortem* 15, p. 118 and *Calendar of Close Rolls* 1377-1381, pp. 262-3.

[21] Much of Great Codham Hall survives from Sir William and Lady Antiocha Coggeshall's time and retains a room which may have been their solar.

Hawkwood's Reputation

[22] A.T.P. Byles, ed., *The Book of the Order of Chyvalry (William Caxton)*, Early English Text Society (1926), p. 123.

[23] S.Basile, ed., *Giovanni Sercambi: Le Illustrazione delle Chroniche nel codice Lucchese. Parte Seconda: Le Illustrazione.* Accademia Lucchese di Scienze, Lettere, Arti: Studi et Testi. 10 (1978), pp. 62 and 87.

[24] College of Arms, Symonds MS, Essex 2. fo. 605r.

[25] For the background to tactics see M. Mallett, 'Mercenaries', in M. Keen, ed., *Medieval Warfare: A History* (1999), pp. 209-29.

[26] Longleat MS (North Muniment Room) 370. The catalogue of manuscripts refers to a letter to Hawkwood with the heading 'Copie des lettres directees a mon Sire Jehan de Haukwode en li art de lastronomie'.

[27] J.R. Lumby, ed., *Polychronicon Ranulphi Higden* 8 (1882), p. 371, and 9 (1886), p. 282. See also V.H. Galbraith, ed., *The Anonimalle Chronicle 1333 to 1381* (1927), p. 56.

[28] Italian proverbial saying.

Hawkwood's Essex

29 O. Rackham, 'The medieval landscape of Essex', in R.H. Allen and R.G. Sturdy, eds, *Archaeology in Essex to AD 1500*, C.B.A. Research Report No. 34 (1980), pp. 103-7 and J.C. Ward, '"Richer in land than in inhabitants": South Essex in the Middle Ages c.1066-c.1340', in K. Neale, ed., *An Essex Tribute* (1987), pp. 97-108.

30 W.J. Rodwell and K. Rodwell, *Historic Churches – A Wasting Asset*, C.B.A. Research Report No. 19 (1977), pp. 4-18. and W.R. Powell, 'The making of Essex parishes', *Essex Review* 62 (1953), pp. 6-18 and 32-41.

31 F. Palgrave, ed., *Parliamentary Writs*, (2 vols, 1827-1834), 2.2, pp. 589-91.

32 For a description of the evolution of the English gentry see N. Saul, *Knights and Esquires: The Gloucestershire Gentry in the Fourteenth Century* (1981) and P. Coss, *Origins of the English Gentry* (2003). For Essex in particular, see also J.C. Ward, *The Essex Gentry and the County Community in the Fourteenth Century*, E.R.O. Studies in Local History 2 (1991).

33 Roskell, Clark and Rawcliffe, *History of Parliament*, 4, pp. 591-93.

34 *Essex Feet of Fines 1182-1547* (4 vols, 1899-1964) and J.C. Ward ed., *The Medieval Essex Community: The Lay Subsidy of 1327*, E.R.O. Publication No. 88 (1983).

35 For the background to Essex agriculture in the fourteenth century see E. Miller, ed., *The Agrarian History of England and Wales 1348-1500* (1991), 3, pp. 53-4, 61, 205, 530, 582, 613-4.

36 C.C. Fenwick, ed., *The Poll Taxes of 1377, 1379 and 1381 Part I Bedfordshire-Lincolnshire*, Records of Social and Economic History New Series 27 (1998), pp. 215-216; Ward, *Medieval Essex Community* and M. Gervers, 'The textile industry in Essex in the late 12th and 13th centuries: a study based on occupational names in charter sources', *E.A.H.* 20 (1989), p.41.

37 M.W. Beresford and H.P.R. Finberg, *English Medieval Boroughs: A Handlist* (1973), pp. 108-11.

38 Ward, *Medieval Essex Community*, pp. 57-69

39 L.R. Poos, 'The rural population of Essex in the later middle ages', *Ec.H.R* 2nd ser. 38 (1985), pp. 515-30.

Hawkwood's Origins

40 M. Gervers, ed., The *Cartulary of Knights of St John of Jerusalem Part I Secunda Camera* (1982), pp. 20-21.

41 Gervers, *St John's Cartulary*, p. 29.

42 E.R.O. T/A 564. (Lay Subsidy for Essex 1319/20).

43 Ward, *Medieval Essex Community.*

44 *Essex Feet of Fines 2 1272-1326* p. 158.

45 Gervers, *St John's Cartulary*, pp. 44-5.

46 F. Palgrave, ed., *Parliamentary Writs* (2 vols, 1827-1834), 2.3, p. 986. Gilbert de Hawkwood manucaptor for John Liston 1324.

47 Ward, *Medieval Essex Community*, p. 63.

48 *Index of Placita de Banco AD 1327-1328* Part 1. P.R.O. Lists and Indexes 32 (1909) p. 144 and E.R.O. D/DCW T 46/3.

49 B.L. Harl. Ch. 51. D.6. (Gilbert de Hawkwood's will 1340).

50 Morant, *History of Essex*, 2, p. 287.

Hawkwood's Family

51 B.L. Harl. Ch. 51. D.6. John de Bousser, who was Rector of Sible Hedingham in 1328, may have baptised John Hawkwood junior (and his siblings). *Index Placita de Banco AD 1327-1328*. Part 1 P.R.O. Lists and Indexes 32 (1909), p. 134.

52 Ward, *Medieval Essex Community*, pp. 63-4.

53 *Essex Feet of Fines 3 1327-1422* p. 72. Sir John Hawkwood's older brother is referred to as 'John Hawkwood of Hedingham the elder' until as late as 1378, see *Essex Fines*, 3, p. 185.

54 According to Morant, John Hawkwood senior, his wife and son, held court in the manor of Bellowes (later Gosfield Hall) in 1344, and it remained in Hawkwood's possession until 1353 when it was known as 'Hawkwood's [manor] Gosfield'. Hawkwood held court at Park Hall, Gosfield in 1360, as did his brother Nicholas in 1363. Morant, *History of Essex*, pp. 378-9.

55 C.R. Starr, 'John Hawkwood the elder of Gosfield: the other John Hawkwood', *Essex Journal* 37 (2002), pp. 49-51.

56 *Calendar of Patent Rolls 1348-1350*, p. 140.

NOTES

Hawkwood's Family continued

[57] *Calendar of Patent Rolls 1377-1381*, p. 277.

[58] *Calendar of Inquisitions Post Mortem* 15, p. 118; and Gervers, *St John's Cartulary*, pp. 121-22.

[59] *Calendar of Close Rolls 1369-74*, pp. 573-4. A deed of February 1370 regarding the sale of land to Sir John Bourchier was signed by 'John de Haukwode [the elder]' E.R.O. D/DCW T33/2.

[60] *Calendar of Inquisitions Post Mortem* 13, p. 92-103; R.C. Fowler, ed., *Registrum Simonis de Sudberia 1326-75* (1927), 1, pp 4-6; and N.H. Nicolas, *Testamenta Vetusta* (1826), 1, p. 87.

[61] *Calendar of Patent Rolls 1401-1405*, pp. 69-70 and 512-13 and *Calendar of Close Rolls 1392-1396*, p. 465; *1396-1399*, p. 351; *1405-1409*, p. 155; *1409-1413*, pp. 387-9; *1413-1419*, p. 2.

[62] W.H. Bliss and J.A. Twemlow, eds, *Calendar of Papal Registers: Papal Letters 1362-1404* (1902), 4, p. 221.

[63] *Essex Fines*, 3, p. 185.

[64] *Calendar of Patent Rolls 1377-1381*, p. 637.

[65] *Calendar of Close Rolls 1377-1381*, pp. 367-8.

[66] ERO D/DPR/5 Rental. *c.*1380 of Colne Priory. The minutely detailed entries in the 40 folios of the book show 'Johes Haukwode' holding land from the priory in Sible Hedingham and Gosfield. (At one point the scribe has interpolated in the Latin text an aphorism in English which begins: 'He that in yowth no vertue wyll use...').

[67] Fenwick, *Poll Taxes*, p. 210 and E.R.O. T/A 565.

[68] E.R.O. D/DBm M164. Rental of Graves Hall, Sible Hedingham 1385, 'Johes Haukwode senior'. The 'John Hawkwode' who on 6 January 1391 witnessed a grant of land in Little Sampford was probably John Hawkwood senior of Gosfield. E.R.O. D/DQ 61/194.

[69] H.J. Rowles, 'The Rikedon Chantry', *Essex Review* 155 (1930), p. 72.

[70] a) E.R.O. D/DU 40/50. b) The John de Hawkwood junior of Finchingfield who, on 23 May 1351 'came into the pasture of Raymond de Lincoln and took a stot belonging to Raymond worth 10s., without Raymond's permission and against the peace, and put the stot to his plough for 3 days', see E.C. Furber, ed., *Essex Sessions of the Peace 1351, 1377-1379*, Essex Archaeological Society Occasional Publications No.3. (1953), p.120, was almost certainly the son of John Hawkwood the elder of Gosfield, rather than his brother as is suggested by F.S. Saunders, *Hawkwood*, (2004), pp. 46-7.

[71] N.A. DL 25/1736.

[72] Morant, *History of Essex*, 1, pp. 378-9.

[73] W.H. Bliss, *Calendar of Papal Registers: Petitions to the Pope 1342-1419* (1896), p. 427.

[74] B.L. Harl. Ch. 51. D.6.

[75] Gervers, *St John's Cartulary*, p. 191.

[76] Morant, *History of Essex*, 1, p. 495.

[77] *Essex Feet of Fines* 1, 1182-1272, p. 211; *Essex Feet of Fines* 2, 1272-1326, p. 169; *Essex Feet of Fines* 3, 1327-1422, p. 103.

[78] *Feudal Aids*, 1284-1431, 2, p. 154.

[79] *Feudal Aids*, 2, pp. 129 and 154.

[80] *Feudal Aids*, 2, p. 218.

[81] *Feudal Aids*, 2, p. 129.

[82] *Feudal Aids*, 2, p. 25.

[83] *Feudal Aids*, 2, p. 163.

[84] *Essex Fines*, 3, pp. 66, 148 and 199.

[85] *Essex Fines*, 3, p. 176.

[86] *Essex Fines*, 2, p. 158.

[87] *Essex Fines*, 3, p. 41.

[88] J.L. Fisher, ed., *Cartularium Prioratus de Colne*, Essex Archaeological Society Occasional Publications No. 1. (1946).

[89] Morant, *History of Essex*, 2, p. 286; *Cartularium Prioratus de Colne*, pp. 2, 3, 18, 23, 31, 35, 38.

[90] *Essex Fines*, 1, p. 197.

[91] *Essex Fines*, 2, p. 47.

[92] *Inquisitions Post Mortem* 10, pp.513-23 and *Inquisitions Post Mortem* 13, pp. 92-103.

Hawkwood's Network

[93] Sir John Hawkwood's coat of arms was argent, a chevron sable with three escallops argent thereon. This is similar to his son-in-law's argent, a cross between four escallops, sable. Hawkwood's seal was a hawk volant with a label issuing from its mouth.

Hawkwood's Network continued

94 *Calendar of Inquisitions Post Mortem* 15, p. 118.

95 *Calendar of Inquisitions Post Mortem* 15, p. 118.

96 *Calendar of Close Rolls* 1377-1381, pp. 262-3.

97 Fenwick, *Poll Taxes*, p. 210.

98 Roskell, Clark and Rawcliffe, *History of Parliament*, 2, pp. 616-18.

99 Fenwick, *Poll Taxes*, p. 210.

100 Roskell, Clark and Rawcliffe, *History of Parliament*, 2, pp. 614-16.

101 J.S. Roskell, 'John Doreward of Bocking Speaker in 1399 and 1413', *E.A.H.* 8 (1976), pp. 209-23.

102 This letter, and another from Hawkwood dated 8 November 1392, together with an indenture of 20 April 1393 were brought before the Lord Mayor and Aldermen of London by Robert Rikedon on 15 June1411. A.H. Thomas, ed., *Calendar of Select Pleas and Memoranda of the City of London 1381-1412* (1932), pp. 308-9.

103 Thomas, *Pleas and Memoranda*, pp. 308-9.

104 'John Edingam, Englishman' witnessed a compact between the Count of Virtue and Sir John Hawkwood dated 1 July 1385, A.B.Hinds, ed., *Calendar of State Papers and Manuscripts existing in the Archives and Collections of Milan* (1912), 1, p. 1.

Hawkwood's Death

105 Temple-Leader and Marcotti, *Sir John Hawkwood*, p. 286.

106 Thomas, *Pleas and Memoranda*, pp. 308-9.

107 Robert Lyndsey, draper of London, left a wife Alice and son John. To the latter he left in his will dated 22 February 1399 his share in 'the great place called 'le ledynhalle'. R.R. Sharpe, ed., *Calendar of Wills Proved and Enrolled in the Court of Hustings* (1890), 2, p. 358.

108 K. Fowler, 'Sir John Hawkwood and the English condottieri in Trecento Italy', *Renaissance Studies* 12 (1998), pp. 131-148 and K. Fowler, *Medieval Mercenaries* (2001).

109 A.H. Thomas, 'Notes on the history of the Leadenhall, A.D. 1195-1488', *London Topographical Record* 13 (1923), pp. 1-22.

110 Temple-Leader and Marcotti, *Sir John Hawkwood*, pp. 276-277.

111 See E. Borsook, *The Mural Painters of Tuscany* (2nd edn, 1980), pp. 74-79 for an account of Paolo Uccello's portrait of Sir John Hawkwood.

112 G. Poggi, *Il Duomo di Firenze* (1988), p. 124. An Italian source provides some evidence that Hawkwood's body was reburied c.1405 under the floor of the Duomo and is quoted in Saunders, *Hawkwood*, pp. 338-9.

113 Temple-Leader and Marcotti, *Sir John Hawkwood*, pp. 293-4.

114 N. Saul, 'The Fragments of the Golafre Brass in Westminster Abbey', *Trans. M.B.S.* 15 Part 1 (1992), pp. 19-32.

115 Temple-Leader and Marcotti, *Sir John Hawkwood*, p. 293-4.

116 Thomas, *Pleas and Memoranda*, pp. 257-8.

117 Thomas, 'Notes on the Leadenhall', pp. 1-22, see also C.M. Barron, 'Richard Whittington: The Man behind the Myth' in A.E.J. Hollaender and W. Kellaway, eds, *Studies in London History: Presented to P.E. Jones* (1969), pp. 197-248.

118 Thomas, *Pleas and Memoranda*, pp. 257-8.

119 a) *Calendar of Patent Rolls* 1408-1413, p. 452. b) For the family of John Coo see Morant, *History of Essex*, 2, p. 307. c) An insight into the complexities of chantry foundations can be found in R. Hill, '"A Chaunterie for Soules": London Chantries in the Reign of Richard II' in F.R.H. Du Boulay and C.M. Barron, eds, *The Reign of Richard II* (1971), pp. 242-55. d) Robert Rikedon had been party to a number of chantry foundations including one for himself and others in Witham church, see H.J. Rowles, 'The Rikedon Chantry', *Essex Review* 155 (1930), p. 72. e) See also the scrapbook which belonged to Lewis Ashurst Majendie of Castle Hedingham which has extensive notes on Sir John Hawkwood, E.R.O. D/DMh/F31. *c.*1700-1927.

120 Morant associates the Hawkwood chantry with present day Hostage Farm (which undoubtedly took its name from the Ostage family of Sible Hedingham): 'The House where the Chantry-priest lived stands at some distance from the Church, and bore then and still bears the name of the Hostage, having originally been a charitable foundation for the entertainment of devout pilgrims. The patronage of this Chantry belonged to the Lord of the maner of Hawkwoods'. Morant, *History of Essex*, 2, pp. 291 and 298.

Hawkwood's Death continued

[121] a) In his description of Hawkwood's tomb at Sible Hedingham, William Holman noted c.1720 that at the 'bottom of the monument where there are several skocheons in stone with the Arms of his military companions depicted on them: but so defaced by time th[a]t they are not discernible enough to distinguish w[ha]t they are', E.R.O. Holman MS T/P 195/12. (b) The illustration of Hawkwood's tomb 'from a drawing taken on the spot 1775' in R. Gough's 'Memoirs of Sir John Hawkwood', *Bibliotheca Topographica Britannica* (1782), 4, pp 1-47, shows an escutcheon charged with a bend cotized – possibly the arms of the Prayers family who held the eponymous manor in Sible Hedingham. c) Morant refers to Oliver and Newenton as Hawkwood's 'military Companions, supposed to be born in the county', *History of Essex* 2 p. 291. d) When Richard Symonds, the Essex antiquary, visited the church in April 1637, he saw the escutcheons, 'at the bottome [of the monument] there are the formes of escochons but the bearings are worne away'. College of Arms, Symonds MS, Essex 2, fo. 605r. e) Morant refers to the Oliver family of Stanway and Thomas Newenton of Sandon, Morant, *History of Essex* 2 pp. 26 and 192. f) John Oliver's connection with the chantry of John Doreward is explored by J.H. Round, 'John Doreward's chantry, Bocking', *T.E.A.S.* New ser. 13 (1915), pp. 73-78.

[122] Sir John's son, John Hawkwood esquire, was named in a licence dated 3 May 1412 to found a chantry in Halstead and in the same year taxed on land he held in Gosfield, Sible Hedingham, Toppesfield and Havering (producing an annual income of fifty pounds). He then disappears from history and is presumed to have died shortly before his patrimony was sold to endow the Hawkwood chantry in 1412. *Feudal Aids* 6 pp. 433-47. For Letters of Administration granted in respect of 'Sir John Hawkwode als Achud' see M. Fitch, ed., *Index to Testamentary Records in the Commissary Court of London* 1374-1488 (1969), 1, p. 93.

Hawkwood's Tomb

[123] *Royal Commission on Historical Monuments: Essex* (4 vols, 1916-23) 1, pp. 266-68 for an architectural description of Sible Hedingham church.

[124] A floor tile showing a 'perching bird, within what would appear to be a diaper pattern in repetition' was found in Holy Trinity church, Bradwell-juxta-Coggeshall and resembles a tile found at Sible Hedingham. They appear to be of late fourteenth century manufacture. W. Rodwell et al, 'Holy Trinity church, Bradwell-juxta-Coggeshall', *E.A.H.* 29 (1998), pp. 110-11.

[125] J. Stow, *The Annales of England* (1605), p. 498.

[126] J. Weever, *Ancient Funerall Monuments* (1631: 1767 edn), p. 381.

[127] College of Arms, Symonds MS, Essex 2, fo. 605r.

[128] a) E.R.O. Holman MS, T/P 95/12. b) Morant refers to the Rector of Sible Hedingham as follows: 'Mr. Moses Cooke, the late worthy Rector here, built a very good Parsonage-house of brick; laid out a handsome garden; and in all respects greatly adorned and improved this Parish.' Morant, *History of Essex*, 2, pp. 291. Cooke was succeeded by Ralph Sneyd as rector on 17 July 1733.

[129] E.R.O. D/Y 1/1/46/7 Moses Cooke to William Holman 23 February 1713.

[130] E.R.O. D/Y 1/1/46/5 Moses Cooke to William Holman 23 April 1713.

[131] E.R.O. Holman MS, T/P 195/12.

[132] Gough's 'Critique of Morant's *History of Essex*' (unpublished) is quoted in W.R. Powell, 'Antiquaries in Conflict: Philip Morant versus Richard Gough', *E.A.H.* 20 (1989), p. 144. Morant, *History of Essex*, 2, pp. 288-90 and R. Gough, 'Memoirs', pp. 1-47.

[133] a) Morant, *History of Essex*, 2, p. 290. b) Morant's descendant, the antiquary C.F.D. Sperling of Dynes Hall, Great Maplestead, knew of Holman's notes on the Hawkwood monument and speculated that 'it would be interesting to know if they [the paintings] still remain beneath the modern colour wash on the wall'. C.F.D. Sperling, 'Sir John Hawkwood', *Essex Review* 39 (1930), pp.72-4.

[134] a) Gough, 'Memoirs', pp.1-47 and Fuller, *Worthies*, 1, p. 513. The minutes of the proceedings of the Society of Antiquaries show that Richard Gough's paper entitled 'Memoirs of the Life of Sir John Hawkwood' was read to the Society over the course of three sessions in 1776. The paper was subsequently printed by John Nichols. b) For the cause of the disagreement between Gough and Morant see Powell, 'Antiquaries in Conflict', pp. 143-6. Morant's "assertion" about the effigies was lifted from Holman's church notes, E.R.O. Holman MS, T/P 195/12.

[135] Gough, 'Memoirs', pp. 30-1

[136] E.R.O. T/A 641/2 church notes of Sir Stephen Glynne c.1867; *Notes and Queries* 9th ser, 10 (1902), p. 50 and B.L. Add. MS, 17460 fo. 152, church notes of David Powell.

[137] F. Chancellor, *Ancient Sepulchral Monuments of Essex* (1890), pp. 123-8.

Hawkwood's Tomb continued

138 National Monuments Record, picture file of Sible Hedingham church. There is a full description of the tomb in M. Tabanelli, *Giovanni Acuto: Capitano di ventura* (1975).

139 N. Coldstream, *The Decorated Style: Architecture and Ornament 1240-1360* (1999).

140 For Sir John Thornbury's career see Roskell, Clark and Rawcliffe, *History of Parliament*, 4, pp. 591-93.

Hawkwood's Posterity

141 Temple-Leader and Marcotti, *Sir John Hawkwood*, pp. 293-4

142 *Notes & Queries* 7th ser. 10 (1890), pp. 101-2.

143 W.H. Bliss and J.A. Twemlow, eds, *Calendar of Papal Registers: Papal Letters* 1362-1404 (1902), 4, p. 191.

144 Grant of denization to 'John, son of John Haukwode, knight' for '40s. paid in the hanaper', *Calendar of Patent Rolls* 1405-1408, p. 276.

145 John Hawkwood junior (son of Sir John) may have never returned to Italy as he was dead by 1412.

146 John Hawkwood junior (son of John the elder).

147 It is doubtful that Sir John even saw his investment property in London and Essex as he was probably in Italy when it was bought by his trustees.

148 *Calendar of Close Rolls* 1405-1409, p. 522.

149 *Calendar of Close Rolls* 1405-1409, p. 522.

150 The grant of 26 September 1409 was "transcribed from the muniments of Mr. C.B. Sperling, of Dynes Hall". C.F.D. Sperling, 'Hawkwood Family', *T.E.A.S.* New ser. 6 (1898), pp. 174-5.

151 a) E.R.O. D/DCW T37/37 a licence dated 3 May 1412 from John Haukwode esquire son of Sir John Haukwode. In 1411, the manor of Graves Hall in Sible Hedingham was purchased by Sir William Coggeshall, Robert Rikedon the elder and John Hereward of Sible Hedingham on behalf of John Hawkwood esquire and his heirs from John Felice of Kedington, Suffolk (who bought it in 1401), *Essex Feet of Fines* 1327-1422 3, pp. 234 and 256. b) The name of the Rector of St Peter's church, Sible Hedingham in 1412 is not known, but it is likely to have been Robert Banbury who was appointed to the living in 1387 under the patronage of the Bourchier family. He is probably identical with Robert, Parson of Sible Hedingham, who as feoffee for the Bourchier family was party to a charter dated at Great Totham on 26 May 1409. R. Newcourt, *Repertorium Ecclesiasticum Parochiale Londinense*, (2 vols, 1708-110), 2, pp. 322-24.

152 *Feudal Aids* 1284-1431, 6, pp. 433-47. An inquisition held at Thaxted on 1 May 1426 following the death of Sir William Coggeshall took evidence regarding a deed dated 14 May 1417 by which Sir William had transferred land in Wethersfield to, amongst others, John Hawkwood (since deceased). If the evidence was accurate (there is now no trace of the deed of 1417) Sir John Hawkwood's son was alive in 1417 but dead by 1426. *Calendar of Inquisitions Post Mortem* 22, pp. 610-11.

153 *Feudal Aids*, 2, p. 230.

154 *Calendar of Patent Rolls* 1388-1392, p. 450.

155 A. Pulling, *The Order of the Coif* (1884), pp. 109-10 and *Calendar of Close Rolls* 1413-1419, p. 216.

156 *Essex Fines*, 3, p. 241.

157 *Calendar of Close Rolls* 1402-1405, pp. 361 and 385.

158 *Calendar of Patent Rolls* 1405-1408, p. 446.

160 *Calendar of Patent Rolls* 1413-1416, p. 270.

161 *Calendar of Patent Rolls* 1413-1416, p. 418.

162 *Calendar of Patent Rolls* 1422-1429, p. 543.

163 Rolf's tomb in Gosfield church is well preserved and incorporates a monumental brass which shows Rolf in the robes and coif of a sergeant-at-law. The brass includes an inscription in Latin which describes him as 'like a flower he shone out among lawyers' and lists his charitable deeds in respect of lepers, poor prisoners and girls wishing to be married. Nearby is the tomb and monumental brass of his son-in-law John Greene, a lawyer of Grays Inn, with an inscription that calls him '[th]e good man of [L]awe [of] Essex'. W. Lack, H.M. Stutchfield and P.W. Whittemore, *The Monumental Brasses of Essex* (2003), pp. 284-7. Thomas Rolf may well have had a chantry priest of his own as the feoffees of his will (they included: Humphrey, Duke of Gloucester; John, Cardinal and Archbishop of York; Thomas, Bishop of Worcester; John, Lord Scrope; William Bourghchier; Richard Neweton, Chief Justice of the Common Pleas; John Carpenter; Thomas Broun; Thomas Payn; Roger Joye; and John

NOTES

Hawkwood's Posterity continued

Pascall) were directed to charge a rent in favour of 'a chaplain in the church of St Katherine Gosfield' against the income from Rolf's manors in 1442. *List of Inquisitions ad Quod Damnum* Part 2, P.R.O. Lists and Indexes 22 (1906), pp. 748.

[164] *Calendar of Patent Rolls 1408-1413*, p. 169.

[165] *Calendar of Patent Rolls 1409-1413*, p. 98.

[166] *Calendar of Inquisitions Post Mortem 19* pp. 207-8.

[167] a) Will of John de Northampton, draper, 1397. R.R. Sharpe, ed., *Calendar of Wills proved and enrolled in the Court of Hustings* 1258-1688 (1890), 2, pp. 333-5. See also V. Hope, *My Lord Mayor* (1989).

[168] E.R.O. D/DU 1280/1 is a pedigree (with illustrations in colour) dated 1589, of the descendants of John and Agnes Greene of Widdington 1400-1589 which includes biographical details of John Greene of Gosfield and Widdington died 1473, Speaker of the Commons.

[169] *Essex Feet of Fines 4 1423-1547*, p. 34.

[170] M. Fitch, ed., *Index to Testamentary Records in the Commissary Court of London 1374-1488* (1969), 1, p. 157. Rolf's principal executors were John Potervile, priest and Thomas Payn, gentleman. See also N.A. CI/106/10. Writ of *diem clausit extremum* after death of Rolf dated 4 July 1440. *Calendar of Fine Rolls* 1437-1445, p. 105.

[171] Rolf's tomb in Gosfield church see F. Chancellor, *Ancient Sepulchral Monuments* (1890), pp. 129-32 and Lack, Stutchfield and Whittemore, *Brasses of Essex*, pp. 284-7.

[172] a) *Calendar of Ancient Deeds* 4 p. 208. b) A list of the inhabitants of Colchester swearing fealty in 1458 includes 'Henricus Hawkewode'. W. Gurney Benham, ed., *The Red Book of Colchester* (1902), p. 80 c) In 1477 Henry Haukwode and his wife Christina were named in a deed. W.G. Benham, ed., *The Oath Book of Colchester* (1907), p. 131. d) For Hawkwood's descendants see J.H. Josselyn 'Sir John Hawkwood, the Condottiere, some of his lineal descendants', *Notes & Queries* 7th ser. 10 (1890), pp. 101-2. e) It is not clear whether the 'Thomas Hawkewode of Kent knight' mentioned in a writ to the sheriffs of London dated 7 March 1409 was a relative of Sir John Hawkwood of Sible Hedingham. *Calendar of Close Rolls* 1405-1409, p. 496.

GLOSSARY

Advowson	The right of presentation of a priest to a benefice.
Affinity	Supporters of a lord on basis of his personal standing.
Aid	Payment due to a lord on special occasions.
Amortise	To transfer land into the inalienable ownership of an ecclesiastical body such as an abbey or priory.
Banneret	Senior knight who commanded other knights.
Capital manor	Manor held directly from the king.
Caput	Principal castle or manor in a feudal estate.
Cartulary	Register of charters, especially titles to land.
Chantry	Chapel endowed for maintenance of a priest to sing masses for the soul of the founder.
Chevauchée	Destructive military raid across enemy territory.
Commission	Group of individuals tasked to perform special duties on behalf of the king.
Common Pleas	Court of common law, mainly concerned with land and debt matters.
Constable	A senior officer in a military formation, responsible for discipline.
Council of Ten	A body set up in an Italian city to deal with issues of treason and other security matters.
Denization	Process by which an alien becomes citizen of a country.
Doge	Chief magistrate or leader in an Italian city.
Enfeoff	To put an individual in possession of land on trust for another.
Escheator	Royal official appointed on yearly basis to administer revenues of the Crown and investigate estates of deceased tenants holding land from the king.
Esquire	Order of gentry ranking immediately below a knight.
Fardel	A fragment, often a quarter.
Fealty	Loyalty sworn to a feudal lord on becoming his/her vassal.
Feet of fines	Tripartite record of fictitious lawsuit in Court of Common Pleas which provided title to land following a change of ownership.
Feoffee	An individual (usually one of several) holding land on trust for another.
Fief	Land granted to a vassal by his/her lord in return for homage and fealty.
Franklin	A landed member of the minor gentry, who could hold county offices such as sheriff, escheator or justice of the peace.
Hundred	Administrative subdivision of a county.
Husbandman	Farmer of small amount of land.
Indult	A licence granted by the Pope to authorise something not usually permitted by church law.
Inquisition post mortem	An investigation into the inheritance of land following the death of the man or woman who held it directly from the king.
Knight of the shire	One of two members of parliament who represented an English county or shire.
Knight's fee	A manor originally granted in exchange for the military service of a knight, but later commuted to a money payment.
Mark	Unit of account representing 160 pence or 13s 4d.
Marshal	Senior officer in a military formation.
Messuage	Portion of land occupied by the site of a dwelling house and its appurtenances.
Pays	Continuous countryside not limited by administrative or territorial boundaries.
Piscina	Stone basin and drain within a wall niche, used for rinsing communion vessels.
Poll tax	A tax levied on every person in an eligible category.

GLOSSARY

Proof of age Inquest	An investigation to establish the age of an heir subsequent to the death of a landowner.
Quitclaim	Discharge, release or renunciation of a claim to land.
Rental	Register of rents due by tenants to a proprietor.
Retinue	Group of military and non military personnel retained in the service of a feudal lord.
Seisin	Feudal possession of land.
Signoria	Governing body in an Italian city.
Slipware	Pottery coated with liquid clay prior to firing.
Stot	A castrated ox; a steer.
Subsidy	A tax granted by parliament to meet special needs of the king.
Tail	Limitation of a freehold estate to a particular class of heirs, usually male.
Toft	Originally a homestead, the site of a house and its outbuildings.
Trecento	Short for *mille trecento*, the fourteenth-century (Italian).
Tribute	Tax paid by one king or city to another as an act of submission or as the price of peace.
Vassal	Someone holding land from a superior lord in return for homage or allegiance.
Villein	A peasant occupier or cultivator entirely subject to a lord or manor.
Wardship	Guardianship and use of income from his or her estate, by feudal lord of an under-age vassal.
Worship	Esteem or respect in which a lord was held by others.
Yeoman	An individual ranking below a gentleman but above a husbandman in the county social hierarchy.
Yoke	Device for hitching animals to a plough.

SELECT BIBLIOGRAPHY

Borsook, E., *The Mural Painters of Tuscany* (2nd edn, 1980).

Bueno de Mesquita, D.M. 'Some condottieri of the Trecento and their relations with political authority', in *Proceedings of the British Academy* 32 (1946), pp. 219-41.

Chancellor, F., *Ancient Sepulchral Monuments of Essex* (1890).

Contamine, P., *War in the Middle Ages* (1984).

Cooper, S., 'An unsung villain. The reputation of a codottiere', *History Today* (Jan., 2006), pp. 19-25.

Fenwick, C.C., ed., *The Poll Taxes of 1377, 1379 and 1381 Part I Bedfordshire - Lincolnshire*, Records of Social and Economic History New Series 27 (1998).

Fowler, K.A., 'Sir John Hawkwood and the English condottieri in Trecento Italy', in *Renaissance Studies* 12 (1998)
'Sir John Hawkwood', *Medieval Mercenaries* [forthcoming] 2 [2008].

Galbraith, V.H., ed., *The Anonimalle Chronicle, 1333 to 1381* (1927).

Gaupp, F., 'The Condottiere John Hawkwood', in *History* New ser., 23 (1938-9), pp. 305-21.

Gervers, M., ed., *The Cartulary of Knights of St. John of Jerusalem Part I Secunda Camera* (1982).

Gough, R., 'Memoirs of Sir John Hawkwood', in *Bibliotheca Topographica Britannia* (1782), 4.

Hector, L.C., and B.F. Harvey, eds, *The Westminster Chronicle, 1381-1394* (1982).

Holmes, G., 'Florence and the Great Schism' *Proceedings of the British Academy* 75 (1989), pp. 291-312.

Jones, T., *Chaucer's Knight* (Revised edn. 1994).

Lack, W., Stutchfield H.M., and Whittmore P.W., *The Monumental Brasses of Essex* (2003).

Lumby, J.R., *Polychronicon Ranulphi Higden* (1882), 2.

Mallett, M., 'Mercenaries' in Keen, M., ed., *Medieval Warfare: A History* (1999).

Morant, P., *The History and Antiquities of the County of Essex* (2 vols, 1763-1768 repr.1978), 2.

Miller, E., ed., *The Agrarian History of England and Wales 1348-1500* (1991), 3.

Prestwich, M., *Armies and Warfare in the Middle Ages: The English Experience* (1996).

Poggi, G., *Il Duomo di Firenze* (1988).

Powell, W.R., 'Antiquaries in conflict: Philip Morant versus Richard Gough', in *E.A.H.* 20 (1989), pp. 143-6.

Roskell, J.S., Clark L., and Rawcliffe C., eds, *The History of Parliament: The House of Commons 1386-1421* (4 vols, 1993).

Saul, N., *Knights and Esquires: The Gloucestershire Gentry in the Fourteenth Century* (1981).

Saunders, F.S., *Hawkwood Diabolical Englishman* (2004).

Sperling, C.F.D., 'Hawkwood Family', in *T.E.A.S.* New ser. 6 (1898), pp. 174-5.
'Sir John Hawkwood', in *Essex Review* 39 (1930), pp. 72-4.

Starr, C.R., 'John Hawkwood the elder of Gosfield: the other John Hawkwood', in *Essex Journal* 37 (2002), pp. 49-51.

Stow, J., *Annales of England* (1631).

Tabanelli, M., *Giovanni Acuto : Capitano di ventura* (1975).

Temple-Leader, J., and Marcotti G., trans. Scott L., *Sir John Hawkwood (L'Acuto): Story of a Condottiere* (1889).

Thomas, A.H., 'Notes on the history of the Leadenhall, A.D.1195-1488', in *London Topographical Record* 13 (1923), pp. 1-22.

Trease, G., *The Condottieri: Soldiers of Fortune* (1970).

Ward, J.C., *The Essex Gentry and the County Community in the Fourteenth Century* E.R.O. Studies in Local History 2 (1991).

Ward, J.C., ed., *The Medieval Essex Community: The Lay Subsidy of 1327*. E.R.O. Publication No 88 (1983).

INDEX